The Workbook on Coping as Christians

The Workbook on Coping as Christians

Maxie Dunnam

UPPER
ROOM BOOKS
NASHVILLE

The Workbook on Coping as Christians

The Upper Room Web Site: http://www.upperroom.org

Photo credits (in order of appearance): Bruce Partain, Mimi Forsyth, David E. Strickler/Strix Pix, Jean-Claude Lejeune, Jean-Claude Lejeune, Florence Sharp.

Scripture quotations not otherwise designated are from the Revised Standard Version of the Bible, copyrighted 1946, 1952, and © 1971 by the Division of Christian Education, National Council of the Churches of Christ in the USA. Used by permission.

Scripture quotations designated PHILLIPS are from *The New Testament in Modern English*, by J. B. Phillips, copyright © 1958 by J. B. Phillips, and are used by permission of the Macmillan Company.

Scripture quotations designated AP are the author's paraphrase.

Excerpts from *From Sad to Glad* by Nathan S. Kline are copyright © 1970 and 1974 by Nathan S. Kline. Reprinted by permission of The Estate of Nathan S. Kline, c/o The Julian Bach Literary Agency, New York.

Excerpts from *The Sanctuary for Lent 1981* and *The Sanctuary for Lent 1983* by Maxie Dunnam are used by permission of Abingdon Press.

Excerpt from "Forgive God?" by V. Gilbert Beers, October 4, 1983, is copyrighted by *Christianity Today* 1983. Used by permission of *Christianity Today*.

Excerpts from "Out of the Depths: Pastoral Care to the Severely Depressed," by Raymond J. Council are used by permission of *Pastoral Psychology*.

Selected lines from "Blood of the Son," by Kenneth Patchen in *The Collected Poems of Kenneth Patchen* are copyright 1945 by Kenneth Patchen. Reprinted by permission of New Directions Publishing Corporation.

"The Lord Is Holding Kirby, After All," by Robert J. Gore is used by permission of the author..

Cover Design: Thelma Whitworth
Cover Transparency: Robert Cushman Hayes
Fifth Printing: September 1998
ISBN: 0-8358-0581-6

Printed in the United States of America

Contents

Introduction

This is a workbook about coping—coping as a Christian. To cope means to "contend or struggle successfully."

Is there anyone who doesn't need resources to help them cope? Every day we are confronted with situations, problems, and relationships that threaten to undo us, to put us down, to defeat us. Yet, I have had some hesitancy about using the word *coping*.

A lot of people are talking about coping. Being who I am—a Christian minister seeking to teach and proclaim the word of God—I am not interested in just a self-help, psychological book. I thought for awhile that I would focus on *conquering* as Christians. Paul wrote to the Christians in Rome, "In all these things we are more than conquerors through him who loved us" (Rom. 8:37).

That is a thrilling word, and there is a sense in which that's what this workbook is about. Yet, as I looked seriously at our predicament and the offer of the Christian gospel, I decided against the use of the word conquering.

To conquer means "subdue, overcome; or crush, to defeat." So, I couldn't use that word exclusively. Why? Some of the issues that I am going to deal with cannot be subdued or crushed or defeated. They are recurring problems in our lives. They are not enemies we are to annihilate or powers we can put down once and for all. They keep coming back, and we have to deal with them from time to time. So *coping* is the right word: "to contend or struggle successfully."

For six weeks we will give our attention to some of our thorniest and most devastating experiences such as depression and death, as well as some of the nitty-gritty, everyday sorts of problems such as loneliness and stress. We want to lift these experiences up, look at them in the light of God's grace with the resources of scriptural guidance, prayer, and our commitment to Christian discipleship, and see if we can't find a way to cope as Christians—to cope in a joyful way which in the end will make us what Paul said we could be as Christians: "more than conquerors." We will move beyond coping to the solid foundation of grace-full, grace-responsive, grace-responsible living.

As I contended in *The Workbook on Spiritual Disciplines,* discipline is an absolute necessity for the Christian life. We may be converted to Christ in the miracle of a moment, but becoming a saint is the task of a lifetime. And we are called to sainthood. We are to *grow up* in Christ (Eph. 4:15), to become mature in Christ (Col. 1:28), and to have the mind of Christ in us (Phil. 2:5). Paul used the metaphor of childbirth to express his groaning desire that Christians grow to the measure of the stature of the fullness of Christ. "Oh, my dear children, I feel the pangs of childbirth all over again till Christ be formed within you" (Gal. 4:19, PHILLIPS).

As Christians we do not emerge full-blown; we grow. We grow by discipline. So the purpose of the workbook is to facilitate the process of coping as a Christian by providing content, ideas for reflection, and guidance for discipline in order that we might appropriate experientially the resources necessary to cope in a meaningful, even joyful, way.

THE PLAN

The plan for this adventure is the same as for my four previous workbooks. It calls for a six-week commitment. It is an individual journey, but my hope is that you will share it with some fellow pilgrims who will meet together once each week during the six weeks of the study. You are asked to give thirty minutes each day to learn about and appropriate ideas and disciplines for coping as a Christian. For most persons these thirty minutes will come at the beginning of the day. However, if it is not possible for you to give the time at the beginning of the day, do it whenever the time is available—but do it regularly. The purpose of this spiritual journey must not be forgotten: to incorporate the content into your daily life.

The workbook is arranged in six major divisions, each designed to guide you for one week. These divisions contain seven sections, one for each day of the week. Each day of the week will have two major aspects: reading about the discipline and reflecting and recording.

In each day's section, you will read something about coping—not too much, but enough to link you with problems, experiences, relationships and situations with which we must cope. Included in this will be some portions of scripture. The scripture is a basic resource for Christian discipline and living. Quotations from most sources other than scripture are followed by the author's name and page number on which the quote can be found. These citations are keyed to the Notes section at the back of the workbook where you will find complete bibliographic information for each source.

Throughout the workbook you will see this symbol ❋ ❋ ❋. When you come to the symbol, *please stop*. Do not read any further. Think and reflect as you are requested to do in order to internalize the ideas being shared or the experience reflected upon.

Reflecting and Recording

Then each day, there will be a time for reflecting and recording. This dimension calls you to record some of your reflections. The degree of meaning you receive from this workbook is largely dependent upon your faithfulness to its practice. You may be unable on a particular day to do precisely what is requested. If so, then simply record that fact and make a note of why you can't follow through. This may give you insight about yourself and help you to grow.

Also, on some days there may be more suggestions than you can deal with in the time you have. Do what is most meaningful for you, and don't feel *guilty.*

The emphasis is upon growth, not perfection. Don't feel guilty if you do not follow exactly the pattern of the days. Follow the content and direction seriously, but not slavishly. Always remember that this is a personal pilgrimage. What you write in your personal workbook is your private property. You may not wish to share it with anyone. For this reason, no two people should attempt to share the same workbook. The importance of what you write is not what it may mean to someone else, but what it means to you. Writing, even if it is only brief notes or single-word reminders, helps us clarify our feelings and thinking.

The significance of the reflecting and recording dimensions will grow as you move along. Even beyond the six-week period, you will find meaning in looking back to what you wrote on a particular day in response to a particular situation.

SHARING WITH OTHERS

In the history of Christian piety, the spiritual director or guide has been a significant person. To varying degrees most of us have had spiritual directors—persons to whom we have turned for support and direction in our spiritual pilgrimage. There is a sense in which this workbook can be a spiritual guide, for you can use it as a private venture without participating in a group.

Its meaning will be enhanced, however, if you share the adventure with eight to twelve others. In this way, the "priesthood of all believers" will come alive, and you will profit from the growing insights of others, and they will profit from yours.

John Wesley believed that "Christian conferencing" was a means of grace for Christians. By Christian conferencing he meant simply Christians sharing intentionally their Christian experience and understanding in deliberate and serious conversation. He designed the "class meeting" as a vehicle for this discipline. In such a fellowship of Christian conversation and shared life, "one loving heart sets another on fire." Your weekly gathering can be that kind of means of grace. A guide for group sharing is included in the text at the end of each week.

If this is a group venture, all persons should begin their personal involvement with the workbook on the same day, so that when you come together to share as a group all will have been dealing with the same material and will be at the same place in the text. It will be helpful if you have an initial get-acquainted group meeting to begin the adventure. A guide for this meeting is provided in this introduction.

Group sessions for this workbook are designed to last one and one-half hours (with the exception of this initial meeting). Those sharing in the group should covenant to attend all sessions unless an emergency prevents attendance. There will be six weekly sessions following this first get-acquainted time.

A group consisting of eight to twelve members is about the right size. Larger numbers limit individual involvement.

One person can provide the leadership for the entire six weeks, or leaders can be assigned from week to week. The leader's task:

- to read directions and determine ahead of time how to handle the session. It may not be possible to use all the suggestions for sharing and praying together. Feel free to select those you think will be most meaningful and those for which you have adequate time.

- to model a style of openness, honesty, and warmth. A leader should not ask others to share what he or she is not willing to share. Usually the leader should be the first to share, especially as it relates to personal experiences.

- to moderate the discussion.

- to encourage reluctant members to participate and try to prevent a few persons from doing all the talking.

- to keep the sharing centered in personal experience, rather than academic debate.

- to honor the time schedule. If it appears necessary to go longer than one and one-half hours, the leader should get consensus for continuing another twenty or thirty minutes.

- to see that meeting time and place are known by all, especially if meetings are held in different homes.

- to make sure necessary materials for meetings are available and that the meeting room is arranged ahead of time.

It is desirable that weekly meetings be held in the homes of the participants. (Hosts or hostesses should make sure there are as few interruptions as possible, e.g., children, telephone, pets, etc.) If meetings are held in a church, they should be in an informal setting. Participants are asked to dress casually, to be comfortable and relaxed.

If refreshments are served, they should come after the formal meeting. In this way, those who wish to stay longer for informal discussion may do so, while those who need to keep to a specific time schedule will be free to leave, but will get the full value of the meeting time.

SUGGESTIONS FOR INITIAL GET-ACQUAINTED MEETING

Since the initial meeting is for the purpose of getting acquainted and beginning the shared pilgrimage, here is a way to get started. (If name tags are needed, provide them.)

1. Have each person in the group give his or her full name and the name by which each wishes to be called. Do away with titles. Address all persons by their first name or nickname. (Each person should make a list of the names somewhere in his/her workbook.)

2. Let each person in the group share one of the happiest, most exciting, or most meaningful experiences he/she has had during the past three or four weeks. After all persons have shared in this way, let the entire group sing the doxology ("Praise God, from Whom All Blessings Flow") or a chorus of praise.

3. After this experience of happy sharing, ask each person who will to share his/her expectations of this workbook study. Why did he or she become a part of it? What does each expect to gain from it? What are the reservations?

4. The leader should now review the introduction to the workbook and ask if there are questions about directions and procedures (this means that the leader should have read the introduction prior to the meeting). If persons have not received copies of the workbook, the books should be handed out now. *Remember that every person must have his/her own workbook.*

5. Day One in the workbook is the day following this initial meeting, and the next meeting should be held on Day Seven of the First Week. If the group must choose another weekly meeting time other than seven days from this initial session, the reading assignment should be brought in harmony with that so that the weekly meetings are always on Day Seven, and Day One is always the day following a weekly meeting.

6. Nothing binds a group together more than praying for one another. The leader should encourage each participant to write the names of each person in the group in his/her workbook, and commit to praying for them by name daily during this six weeks.

7. After checking to see that everyone knows the time and place of the next meeting, the leader may close with a prayer, thanking God for each person in the group, for the opportunity of growth, and for the possibility of growing through spiritual disciplines.

Note: If someone in the group has an instant camera, bring it to the group meeting next week. Be prepared to take a picture of each person in the group to be used as an aid to prayer.

Interruptions and Limitations

Day One: *Just When We Think We're Safest*

One day Leonardo da Vinci was working on the face of Jesus in his masterpiece, the "Last Supper." For twelve years he had been working on the painting, and much of it had been completed. There was a blank space where the face of Jesus was to appear. For inspiration, Leonardo had one of his pupils read the thirteenth chapter of John's gospel. That is the chapter that tells of Jesus, when he was having that last supper with his disciples, taking a basin and a towel, washing the disciples' feet, and dramatically living out who he was.

Hardly had the sound of the last word of the gospel story died away when the image of Jesus, that face full of life, began to form in Leonardo's mind. Just then another pupil burst into the room and cried out, "At last, we've found you. We've come from the Duchess."

"What has happened?" Leonardo asked.

"Trouble, Monsieur Leonardo! The pipes in the bath will not work," replied the pupil.

"Nonsense," said da Vinci. "You see that I'm busy. Find Zorra Astro and tell him to fix the pipes."

"Oh no," the pupil declared. "I'm ordered by the Duchess not to return without you."

Leonardo tried to resume his work, but it was no use. The image was gone. He slowly closed his box of colors and descended the scaffold, leaving off painting the face of Jesus to go and fix the plumbing.

That's the way it is, isn't it? When all is going well, there is an interruption. A significant task to which we are committed has to be deserted when we are diverted by some mundane requirement. This is a good place for us to begin our work on coping because nothing is more

15

common and nothing more irksome. The poet Robert Browning wrote in "Bishop Blougram's Apology":

> Just when we are safest, there's
> a sunset-touch,
> . . . someone's death,
> A chorus ending from Euripides,
> And that's enough for fifty hopes
> and fears.

Browning was talking about profound, life-shattering interruptions such as death with which we will deal later, yet his picture is a good one for all interruptions. Just when we're settled down, when we're safest, when we think everything is going along smoothly, there's an interruption, a "sunset touch": divorce, loss of job, a serious accident, a transfer in our job that takes us to a strange city, severe financial reversal, an illness (your own or that of a family member), a disruption in relationships that demands a lot of attention.

Reflecting and Recording

Stop for a moment now and look back over the past three or four months. List any interruptions that you would label serious.

Look at your list now. Which was the *most* serious? Recall as much as you can about that one serious interruption. Did it disrupt your life? Make you mad? Drain you of energy? Affect relationships and/or job performance? Write a paragraph about what happened, your feelings and responses.

Read and ponder this word of scripture.

> The Lord created me at the beginning of his work,
>   the first of his acts of old.
> Ages ago I was set up,
>   at the first, before the beginning of the earth.
> When there were no depths I was brought forth,
>   when there were no springs abounding with water.
> Before the mountains had been shaped,
>   before the hills, I was brought forth;
> before he had made the earth with its fields,
>   or the first of the dust of the world.
> When he established the heavens, I was there
>   when he drew a circle on the face of the deep,
> when he made firm the skies above,
>   when he established the fountains of the deep,
> when he assigned to the sea its limit,
>   so that the waters might not transgress his command,
> when he marked out the foundations of the earth,
>   then I was beside him, like a master workman;
> and I was daily his delight,
>   rejoicing before him always,
> rejoicing in his inhabited world
>   and delighting in the sons of men.
>   —Proverbs 8:22–31

The scripture writer reminds us of who we are—persons with an eternal destiny, persons with a life *in* God.

Ponder for a few minutes what such a vision of self might do for us as we live daily with interruptions.

❄   ❄   ❄

During the Day

When an interruption comes today—any interruption, serious or slight—remember the eternal time line of God in which you are set, and try to see how *limited* the interruption is.

Day Two: *Presiding over Interruptions*

Norman Cousins once described his work as editor of *The Saturday Review* as "presiding over interruptions."

Do you feel that you spend your life presiding over, trying to manage, trying to keep going in a primary direction, when you're pulled hither and yon by interruptions?

This is one of the most troublesome flies in the ointment of life. These interruptions don't announce themselves. The seriousness of them is dependent upon the nature of the interruption, but also on what is going on in our lives when they pop in.

Yesterday you listed some serious interruptions you experienced during the past few months. These serious interruptions don't come often for most of us, but there are the slight ones which are as common as corn flakes. They irritate us and play havoc with our schedules, our relationships, our jobs, and our energy.

Less serious interruptions might include a telephone call when we're rushing out the door for an important engagement, the guests who come unannounced, the loss of electric power when we're making final preparations for a dinner party, having to pick up a child at school unexpectedly because of a stomach ache, and the list could go on and on.

If we don't learn to cope even with these slight interruptions, they will keep our nerves frayed, will drain us of the energy we need to invest more meaningfully, will drive us to distraction and disrupt important relationships.

The interruptions are not going to go away. They will keep popping up to invade our routine. Life is just that way. Jesus knew about interruptions. Here is a case in point.

The apostles returned to Jesus, and told him all that they had done and taught. And he said to them, "Come away by yourselves to a lonely place, and rest a while." For many were coming and going, and they had no leisure even to eat. And they went away in the boat to a lonely place by themselves. Now many saw them going, and knew them, and they ran there on foot from all the towns, and got there ahead of them. As he went ashore he saw a great throng, and he had compassion on them, because they were like sheep without a shepherd; and he began to teach them many things.

—Mark 6:30–34

This passage follows a period of intense ministry for Jesus. If you go back to chapter 5 in Mark's gospel you will read the story of the demoniac in the cemetery, whom Jesus ministered to, leaving him "clothed and in his right mind" (Mark 5:15). You would read of a ruler of the synagogue, Jairus, coming to Jesus, falling at Jesus' feet and begging him to come and heal his daughter who was at the point of death, and Jesus responding. You would read that marvelous story of faith about a woman who had had a flow of blood for twelve years, pressing through the multitude and touching just the hem of his garment, and Jesus feeling that touch and responding to that woman's faith: "Daughter, your faith has made you well; go in peace and be healed of your disease" (Mark 5:34).

Following that period of intense ministry and his sending his own disciples out to minister, Jesus realized that all of them needed rest and renewal. So he suggested that they cross the Sea of Galilee and find an isolated place where they could rest, be silent, share and pray together. But as they make their way to that place of retreat, people find out where he is going, interrupt him, and it happens again. Jesus is cast into the pressing demand of human needs.

From Jesus we can learn that we do not have to allow interruptions to play havoc with our lives. We can, instead, meaningfully integrate them into our lives.

Jesus could integrate interruptions into his life because he had a clear purpose. His vocation, what he was about, was the connecting, integrating power in his life. This is our guidance: *to cope with interruptions we must have a purpose and keep that purpose clear.*

The power of purpose was so evident in Jesus. He never lost sight of that purpose. He had settled it at the outset when he spent forty days and nights in the wilderness. He would not be a magician, turning stones into bread. He would not be a power broker, ruling over nations. He would not be a superstar, attracting attention to himself by jumping off the mountainside. He stated his purpose clearly: "The Son of man also came not to be served but to serve" (Mark 10:45). Not even when he was at the center of everyone's attention did he lose sight of his purpose.

Reflecting and Recording

In the left column, list five or six different "slight" interruptions you experienced during the past two or three days.

Interruption   Response

Beside each interruption make notations about your feelings in response to them, the time you felt you lost, diversion of interest and focus. Did you find it hard to get back "on track"? If it was a person who interrupted you, how did you feel about the person? Did you express or suppress your feelings? Make those notations now.

✳   ✳   ✳

Tomorrow we will look at another lesson from Jesus for coping. For now ask yourself the question: Were I clearer in my vocation and purpose would slight interruptions such as these I have just considered, or even the serious ones such as I listed yesterday, be so diverting and devastating?

During the Day

We can control our response to slight interruptions by simply paying attention. Are persons involved who need my caring? Does this situation deserve the time I am giving it? Can I center my thinking here for a time, leaving my other involvement, so that I will not be confused or drained of energy by seeking to keep my mind in two places? Is what I am being taken from more important than what I am being pulled to?

Let each interruption have enough attention to clarify perspective and purpose.

Day Three: *Persons, Not Things, Are of Ultimate Value*

When Jesus had crossed again in the boat to the other side, a great crowd gathered about him; and he was beside the sea. Then came one of the rulers of the synagogue, Jairus by name; and seeing him, he fell at his feet, and besought him, saying, "My little daughter is at the point of death. Come and lay your hands on her, so that she may be made well, and live." And he went with him.

And a great crowd followed him and thronged about him. And there was a woman who had had a flow of blood for twelve years, and who had suffered much under many physicians, and had spent all that she had, and was no better, but rather grew worse. She had heard the reports about

Jesus, and came up behind him in the crowd and touched his garment. For she said, "If I touch even his garments, I shall be made well." And immediately the hemorrhage ceased; and she felt in her body that she was healed of her disease. And Jesus, perceiving in himself that power had gone forth from him, immediately turned about in the crowd, and said, "Who touched my garments?" And his disciples said to him, "You see the crowd pressing around you, and yet you say, 'Who touched me?'" And he looked around to see who had done it. But the woman, knowing what had been done to her, came in fear and trembling and fell down before him, and told him the whole truth. And he said to her, "Daughter, your faith has made you well; go in peace, and be healed of your disease."

—Mark 5:21–34

This is one of the most thrilling stories in all the New Testament. The story is of a healing that takes place on the way to a healing. This is one of the many interruptions in Jesus' life. He was on his way to heal Jairus's daughter when, in the midst of the jostling crowd, he sensed something going on, someone was touching him. What a bold thing this woman had done! What wild abandonment in faith and trust—just to touch the hem of Jesus' garment. She did, and Jesus did—he healed her.

We can cope with our interruptions and integrate them positively into our lives if we keep the perspective that persons, not things, are the eternal value. With that perspective, we realize that life and love are "interruptable." So a phone call comes when we are grappling with a serious problem. So there's a knock on our door in the middle of the morning when we're rushing around trying to get ready for a very important engagement. So a call comes at midnight when we desperately need our rest for the work we are to do tomorrow. When we have the right perspective on persons, life and love are interruptable.

I had a marvelous Methodist minister friend out in Southern California. His name was Skidmore. We called him Skid. When he was fifty-one years old, his doctors diagnosed an inoperable cancer and gave him six months to a year to live. He wrote the following letter to his congregation.

Dear Christian friends,

It has taken me 51 years of living and 33 years in the Christian life to learn the real meaning of Jesus' word in the Sermon on the Mount, "Do not be anxious about tomorrow." I have been a very ambitious man, and I have abhorred the mediocre. Always within me has been the desire to excel. In living this way I have been impatient and anxious, inattentive and often unkind. My goals have been long distance and compulsive. In consequence, I have given less than my best to the person in front of me, because I was thinking way ahead to the goals and plans beyond. Now all is different. My anxieties are gone. I have no idea how long I shall live, *but then there is today.* Each day is meaning more to me than ever before. Each person I meet can have all there is of me than ever before. Each person I meet can have all there is of me for those moments we're together. I may not get as much done from here on out, but life is far more peaceful. I have at last come to accept these words of Jesus *as* for me, "Don't be anxious about your life."

I like that one sentence: "Each person I meet can have all there is of me for those moments we're together." Life and love are interruptable.

We need to learn from Skid. The interruption of cancer did not defeat him. He clarified his purpose, and he regained the perspective that persons, not things, are of ultimate value.

Reflecting and Recording

List here again those serious interruptions you listed on Day One.

Looking back at how you handled those interruptions, would there have been any difference if your purpose had been clearer, if you had been more committed to the perspective that persons, not things, are of ultimate value? Make some notes here about the difference there might have been.

During the Day

Make a commitment that today "each person I meet can have all there is of me for those moments we're together."

Day Four: *When Nature Says No to Some Yes in You*

> You who keep account
> Of crisis and transition in this life,
> Set down the first time Nature says plain ''no''
> To some ''yes'' in you, and walks over you
> In gorgeous sweeps of scorn. We all begin
> By singing with the birds, and running fast
> With June days, hand in hand: but once, for all,
> The birds must sing against us, and the sun
> Strike down upon us like a friend's sword caught
> By an enemy to slay us, while we read
> The dear name on the blade which bites at
>   us!—
> That's bitter and convincing: after that,
> We seldom doubt that something in the
>   large
> Smooth order of creation, . . .
>   has gone wrong.

> —Elizabeth Barrett Browning
> ''Aurora Leigh''

It is a brilliant image: when ''Nature says plain 'no' to some 'yes' in you.'' Most of us don't live very long before that happens, when nature ''walks over [us] in gorgeous sweeps of scorn.'' That's a big part of what it means to be human. So we have to live with *limitations* as well as interruptions.

There are dramatic cases:

- An auto accident maims a brilliant young man, and sends his career careening in a wildly different direction, or no direction at all.
- A birth defect limits a baby for life.
- A tornado wipes out a community.
- Business failure wrecks the security of a family.
- The birth of a child, by unfortunate events in the process, leaves the mother paralyzed and in a wheelchair for life.
- A disease claims a beloved wife when she is only forty-two.

We could go on and on, but the picture is a dark and dreadful one at which we have looked often and been mystified. So we don't need to paint a picture. The picture is life itself, Nature saying ''no'' to some ''yes'' within us.

Here is part of Paul's story:

I must boast; there is nothing to be gained by it, but I will go on to visions and revelations of the Lord. I know a man in Christ who fourteen years ago was caught up to the third heaven—whether in the body or out of the body I do not know, God knows. And I know that this man was caught up into Paradise—whether in the body or out of the body I do not know, God knows—and he heard things that cannot be told, which man may not utter. On behalf of this man I will boast, but on my own behalf I will not boast, except of my weaknesses. Though if I wish to boast, I shall not be a fool, for I shall be speaking the truth. But I refrain from it, so that no one may think more of me than he sees in me or hears from me. And to keep me from being too elated by the abundance of revelations, a thorn was given me in the flesh, a messenger of Satan, to harass me, to keep me from being too elated. Three times I besought the Lord about this, that it should leave me; but he said to me, "My grace is sufficient for you, for my power is made perfect in weakness." I will all the more gladly boast of my weaknesses, that the power of Christ may rest upon me. For the sake of Christ, then I am content with weaknesses, insults, hardships, persecutions, and calamities; for when I am weak, then I am strong.

—2 Corinthians 12:1–10

We don't know what Paul's thorn was. We don't need to know. It was a chronic problem that plagued him to his death. He never got rid of it but found grace to live with it, to triumph over it.

Reflecting and Recording

What has been the most difficult and painful experience in your life of nature saying no to some yes within you? Get the experience clearly in mind. Describe it and your feelings about it, writing enough to recapture the essence of it.

Paul heard the Lord say, "My grace is sufficient for you." In the experience described above, was there any hint or revelation of God's grace? Be honest and write a few sentences about it.

During the Day

Memorize this line of scripture: "My grace is sufficient for you, for my power is made perfect in weakness." This is the Lord's word to us not only for our extreme difficulties, but for our daily life in its sameness and routine. Take that promise with you into the day.

Day Five: *There Is a Tragic Dimension to Life*

How do we cope with nature saying no to some yes within us? How do we live with life's limitations?

What I offer for consideration today is not enough of an answer, but it is a partial answer and where we must begin. *We must simply accept the fact that there is a tragic dimension to life.*

Sometimes this tragic dimension is like a mocking demon that arrogantly challenges the idea we all seek to hold firmly in our minds: God is good and intends good for everyone.

Such a mocking challenge came in the stroke of Bishop Gerald Kennedy. He was one of my heroes, one of the most colorful and effective preachers of the twentieth century. He made the cover of *Time* magazine and few preachers do that.

I used to drive for hundreds of miles to hear him preach whenever he would come to the Southeast. He took a personal interest in me and other young ministers who sought to make what we thought was a solid Christian witness in the racial upheaval in Mississippi in the 1960s. It was because of him that I moved to California in 1964.

What a preacher! A word craftsman, eloquent in his crisp clarity, pungent with his images and powerful in his perceptive interpretation of scripture.

Then it happened. A stroke left him almost completely unable to make understandable sounds. What a mockery of fate! What a tragic instance of nature saying no to some yes within us. It was a terrible irony that the very talent with which he was uncommonly gifted was taken away by that one fell blow of nature. For the last ten years of his life, he could not preach, and, for the most part, could not even speak.

A preacher friend, Erwin Trotter, reminded us in an article he wrote when Bishop Kennedy died that in the first book of sermons the bishop ever published, he included a sermon entitled "The Half-Witted Brother." I went back and reread that sermon as I worked on this section. It was on the theme of unexplained evil and suffering. Bishop Kennedy used the philosophy of an African tribe: Although God is good and wishes good for everybody, unfortunately he has a half-witted brother who is always interfering with what God does. Images are not to be taken literally but for the powerful truth they suggest. There is a tragic dimension to life: a half-witted brother is always messing up what God seeks to do. Nature is always saying no to some yes within us and sometimes walks over us "in gorgeous sweeps of scorn."

We can't help it. We ask why and we seek reasons for the inevitable tragic edges of life.

In the Old Testament, the Jews understood that God was responsible for everything—the good and the bad—so they reduced life to a simple formula. When we are good, good comes to us; when we are bad, bad comes.

That doesn't satisfy us because it is true neither to scripture nor experience. The rain falls on the just and the unjust. Still we seek an answer.

The most reasonable effort at explaining pain and suffering I know is Leslie Weatherhead's small but great book, *The Will of God*. Weatherhead talked about the intentional will of God, the circumstantial will of God, and the ultimate will of God in an effort to explain some of the things that go on in life. That is a good way to explain it as far as reason goes. It is helpful to our rational selves.

But as rational as we may be about it all, reason does little for our hurting hearts when nature says no to some yes within us. However we explain it, whatever reasons come forth, and no matter how convincing our theories, when we press the issue, God does have to at least *allow* things, and we can't escape that. So our hearts continue to hurt.

We are pushed back to that hard place of simply accepting the unexplainable, sometimes irrational, fact that there is a tragic dimension to life. While we may reason about it in a satisfactory way, our reasoning does not alleviate the pain.

Reflecting and Recording

Spend a few minutes with Paul's affirmation.

We have this treasure in earthen vessels, to show that the transcendent power belongs to God and not to us. We are afflicted in every way, but not crushed; perplexed, but not driven to despair; persecuted, but not forsaken; struck down, but not destroyed; always carrying in the body the death of Jesus, so that the life of Jesus may also be manifested in our bodies. For while we live we are always being given up to death for Jesus' sake, so that the life of Jesus may be manifested in our mortal flesh. So death is at work in us, but life in you. . . .

So we do not lose heart. Though our outer nature is wasting away, our inner nature is being renewed every day. For this slight momentary affliction is preparing for us an eternal weight of glory beyond all comparison, because we look not to the things that are seen but to the things that are unseen; for the things that are seen are transient, but the things that are unseen are eternal.

—2 Corinthians 4:7–12, 16–18

During the Day

"So we do not lose heart." Call this word to mind as you greet every difficult experience today.

Day Six: *God Uses Suffering for Our Good and God's Glory*

We closed yesterday by reflecting on Paul's testimony. Begin today by reflecting on a part of that testimony as Clarence Jordan paraphrases it. "Just look! We catch it from every direction but don't let them squeeze the life out of us. We don't know which end is up, but they don't upend us. We are persecuted but never wiped out. We are banged all over, but they don't get rid of us" (Jordan, pp. 79–80).

That is picturesque and powerful language. In the more traditional translation Paul identifies the bottom line: "So we do not lose heart. Though our outer nature is wasting away, our inner nature is being renewed every day" (2 Cor. 4:16). With that affirmation stirring in our hearts, we press the question. How do we cope with life's limitations, with nature saying no to some yes within us?

A dramatic step of faith is essential. It is the revelation of faith which tells us that God doesn't get rid of suffering but uses suffering for our good and God's glory. This isn't easy, but once grasped and held on to, it enables us to cope.

A week preceding this writing, I talked with a woman who has cancer. She has had it now for about six years. She is not in remission and is taking chemotherapy each week. She has kept a journal for ten years. The past three and one-half years have been a deliberate spiritual journal as she has plotted her journey, her walk with Christ as she has walked with cancer.

She is a radiant woman. There's sort of a glow about her. Her eyes sparkle as she tells of the good that has come from nature saying no to the yes in her. Not the least good has been the dramatic conversion of her son, his redemption from drugs, and his present ministry with drug victims.

She is certain that good for her and glory to God has come from her illness. Now God did not afflict her with that dread disease but God has used it. You and I can count on that, too. God doesn't rid us of our suffering but uses it for our good and God's glory.

Reflecting and Recording

Go back to Day Four and read what you wrote about the most difficult and painful experience of nature saying no to some yes within you. Examine that experience now to see if any good has come from it, any glory for God.

✳   ✳   ✳

If not any in that experience, can you think of another "tragic" experience in which you were involved where good came to you and/or others and glory to God? Make some notes about that experience here. Name it and record what happened.

During the Day

Is there someone you know who is presently going through a tough experience? Call that person by phone or write a letter of love and encouragement. Tell him or her what you are doing with this workbook and how you are seeking ways of coping.

Day Seven: *Resist Self-Pity and Visualize a New Possibility*

It is so easy when nature says no to some yes in our life to give way to self-pity, one of the most debilitating of all emotions. Christians are saved from self-pity by the remembrance that Christ never allowed his soul to be cornered into despair, and Paul followed in Jesus' steps: "Though our outer nature is wasting away, our inner nature is being renewed every day" (2 Cor. 4:16).

Therefore, though self-pity is inviting, resist it. And the second part of this word of guidance is: *Visualize a new possibility.* This provides great help in coping with life's limitations.

I firmly believe that our big problem is that we *want* something different to happen in our lives, but we really don't *expect* it to happen. Do you get the point I'm making?

There is a difference, a vast difference, between *wanting* things to be different and *expecting* them to be different. The Bible doesn't merely hold up the possibility that things may be different; the hope offered by the Bible is that you can fully expect things to be different. The big word is this: Self-pity is inviting, but resist it and visualize a new possibility.

In 1958 Liu Shih-kun was nineteen years old when he won second prize in the First International Tchaikovsky Piano Competition. Van Cliburn won first place and gained immediate worldwide recognition. Liu Shih-kun returned to China, forgotten by the rest of the world. He became an established concert pianist in China, but during the Cultural Revolution he was imprisoned for refusing to renounce the music of the Western world.

While imprisoned, he was beaten mercilessly. From the assault, the bone in his right forearm was cracked. For the next six years, he sat in a tiny prison cell. He had no books except the teaching of Mao, no paper on which to write, and no piano. Then Richard Nixon built a diplomatic bridge across the Pacific Ocean and the prison door opened for Liu. An imprisoned concert pianist would have been an embarrassment to the

People's Republic. Liu was released from jail and ordered to perform in Peking with the Philadelphia Orchestra. This "request" was from Madame Chiang Ching, the woman who had ordered his incarceration and beatings in the first place. To everyone's surprise, Liu played flawlessly! After the concert, he was again imprisoned for another eighteen months. He was released once more, ordered to perform, and again played brilliantly!

Liu Shih-kun never returned to prison after that; the political and cultural climate of China was changing. He is finally recognized in his homeland as a very gifted musician. But the fact that he had twice before played as though he had never stopped is astounding! For when Liu was imprisoned, all things musical belonging to him were destroyed. In prison he had been denied a piano and even paper which might have allowed him to recapture the music he had lost.

Yet, something was left in Liu Shih-kun that prison guards could not take away—his reason for living: his love of music. In a tiny prison for seven and a half years, Liu Shih-kun visualized a new possibility. He practiced his beloved music in his vivid imagination—on a piano that no one else could see!

His music was as real and driving a force while he was imprisoned as it ever had been. The government of China tried to change Liu, to kill his spirit, but he refused to be defeated or give in to self-pity. He kept visualizing a new possibility and would not be limited by the awful limitations placed upon him (Paraphrased. Aurandt, pp. 18–20).

Reflecting and Recording

Are you facing some difficult situation now? Describe that situation in one or two sentences.

Are you tending to self-pity? Can you visualize a new possibility? Stay with your thinking for a few minutes.

※ ※ ※

Let this word of Paul encourage you.

Rejoice in the Lord always; again I will say, Rejoice. Let all men know your forbearance. The Lord is at hand. Have no anxiety about anything, but in everything by prayer and supplication with thanksgiving let your requests be made known to God. And the peace of God, which passes all understanding, will keep your hearts and your minds in Christ Jesus.

Finally, brethren, whatever is true, whatever is honorable, whatever is just, whatever is pure, whatever is lovely, whatever is gracious, if there is any excellence, if there is anything worthy of praise, think about these things. What you have learned and received and heard and seen in me, do; and the God of peace will be with you.

—Philippians 4:4–9

During the Day

Determine now that you are going to resist every pull toward self-pity that comes today—no matter what happens.

Group Meeting for Week One

Note to group leader: Locate a Polaroid camera. Maybe someone in the group has one if you don't. Take to this group meeting.

Introduction

These group sessions will be most meaningful as they reflect the experience of all the participants. This guide is simply an effort to facilitate personal sharing. Therefore, do not be rigid in following these suggestions. The leader, especially, should seek to be sensitive to what is going on in the lives of the participants and to focus the group sharing on those experiences. Ideas are important. We should wrestle with new ideas as well as with ideas with which we disagree. It is important, however, that the group meeting not become a debate about ideas. The emphasis should be on persons—experiences, feelings, and meaning.

The very fact that you are addressing the subject of *coping* is witness to the fact that you are struggling. The sooner and more freely each person shares personally, the more helpful you will be to each other. As the group comes to the place where all can share honestly and openly what is happening in their lives, the experience will become increasingly meaningful.

Sharing Together

1. You may begin your sharing together by allowing time for each person in the group to share his or her most meaningful day with the workbook this week. The leader should begin this sharing. Tell why that particular day was so meaningful.

2. Now share your most difficult day. Tell what you experienced and why it was so difficult.

3. On Day Six, you were asked to consider the fact that God uses suffering for our good and God's glory. Ask someone to share an experience of suffering that resulted in his or her good. Ask another to share an experience of difficulty, tragedy, or suffering that brought glory to God.

Praying Together

Each week the group is asked to pray together. Corporate prayer is one of the great blessings of Christian community. There is power in corporate prayer, and it is important that this dimension be included in our shared pilgrimage.

It is also important that you feel comfortable in this and that no pressure be placed on anyone to pray aloud. *Silent* corporate prayer may be as vital and meaningful as verbal corporate prayer.

God does not need to hear our verbal words to hear our prayers. Silence, where thinking is centered and attention is focused, may provide our deepest periods of prayer. There is power, however, in a community on a common journey verbalizing their thoughts and feelings to God in the presence of their fellow pilgrims.

Verbal prayers should be offered spontaneously as a person chooses to pray aloud—not ''let's go around the circle now, and each one pray.''

Suggestions for this ''praying together'' time will be given each week. The leader for the week should regard these only as suggestions. What is happening in the meeting—the mood, the needs that are expressed, the timing—should determine the direction of the group praying together. Here are some possibilities for this closing period.

1. Let the group think back over the sharing that has taken place during this session. What personal needs or concerns came out of the sharing? Ask the group to verbalize the needs and concerns that have been expressed. Don't hesitate to mention a concern that you may have picked up from another, i.e., ''Mary isn't able to be with us this week because her son is in the hospital. Let's pray for her son and for her.''

It will be helpful for each person to make notes of the concerns and needs that are mentioned. Enter deliberately into a period of silence. Let the leader verbalize each of these needs successively, allowing for a brief period following each so that persons in the group may center their attention and focus their prayers on the person, need, or concern mentioned. All of this will be in silence as each person prays in *his* or *her own way*.

2. Let the leader close this time of sharing and silent prayer by asking the group to share in a prayer liturgy. The leader will call the name of each person in the group, after which the group will say, ''Lord, bless him/her'' as they focus their eyes on that person. Let the person whose name is called look at each person in the room to catch their eye and receive their ''look'' of blessing as well as their word. When this is done, the leader calls the next name, until all are ''blessed'' and looked at with a blessing. Then the leader may simply say, ''Amen.''

Picture Taking: Before everyone leaves, take a picture of each person. Turn the pictures face down on table and let each person take one. This is the person for whom you will pray specifically this week. Before you go, take a few minutes to visit with the person whose picture you chose, getting to know him/her better. Ask if there are things coming up in that person's life about which you might pray. Return the pictures each week, shuffle them face down, and let each person select a new ''face'' for whom to pray.

Worry, Guilt, and Fear

Day One: *To Worry or Not to Worry*

As we begin, let's touch base with the situation. There is a good picture of it in one of Charles Schulz's *Peanuts* cartoons. Snoopy, the hilarious hound, is flat on his back on top of his good old doghouse. He is not so hilarious today but rather ponderous. "Rats!" he cries. Now he sits up and continues, "How can I sleep knowing that any moment a wolf could come by and blow my house down." Leaning over the roof, he says, "Life has too many worries . . . today it's wolves . . ." And pulling out his tennis racket, he cries, "Yesterday, it was my backhand!"

I don't know anybody who doesn't have something to worry about. There are occasions when worry is not only acceptable but needed. There is no shortage of concerns about which we may legitimately worry. Writing in *Piedmont Airlines* magazine, Bishop Ernest A. Fitzgerald shared the following: "Several years ago, one of America's greatest humorists wrote a book in which she made an interesting confession, 'I am an orthodox worrier. There are days when everything seems to go right. Such days nearly drive me nuts.'"

Not many people are candid enough to make that kind of confession. We confess about worrying when everything goes wrong, but when everything goes right and we still worry—we don't like to talk about that.

There is no question about it, worry has a major place in most of our lives. And like so many emotional problems, worry can play havoc with us. It requires coping skills. There is a chronic, crippling worry that is altogether debilitating, and we must learn to manage it.

But there is also a legitimate worry. I don't know how long ago it was, but I remember, and perhaps some of you do, when many TV stations, just before the eleven o'clock news, would have a voice come on saying, "It's eleven o'clock; do you know where your children are?" Well, if you had agreed with your children that they would come in at twelve, you would not be worried. However, if the night stretched on, and it was three o'clock in the morning, then you would be concerned, and you should be. You would begin to worry, and that would be a constructive act. So, we want to begin our work on coping with worry by acknowledging the fact that worry can be constructive.

Look at a brief section from Jesus' Sermon on the Mount.

> Therefore I tell you, do not be anxious about your life, what you shall eat or what you shall drink, nor about your body, what you shall put on. Is not life more than food, and the body more than clothing? Look at the birds of the air: they neither sow nor reap nor gather into barns, and yet your heavenly Father feeds them. Are you not of more value than they? And which of you by being anxious can add one cubit to his span of life? And why are you anxious about clothing? Consider the lilies of the field, how they grow; they neither toil or spin; yet I tell you, even Solomon in all his glory was not arrayed like one of these. But if God so clothes the grass of the field, which today is alive and tomorrow is thrown into the oven, will he not much more clothe you, O men of little faith? Therefore, do not be anxious, saying, ''What shall we eat?'' or ''What shall we drink?'' or ''What shall we wear?'' For the Gentiles seek all these things; and your heavenly Father knows that you need them all. But seek first his kingdom and his righteousness, and all these things shall be yours as well.
>
> —Matthew 6:25–33

Can there be any question about Jesus' teaching? We are not to worry. Yet, a moment ago I suggested that we begin our work on coping with worry by acknowledging the fact that worry can be constructive. We need to set Jesus' particular word about worry in the Sermon on the Mount in the context of his total teaching. Any virtue, pressed too far, can be a distortion, leading to negative not positive action and result in our lives.

If anything is worse than taking life too seriously, it is taking life too lightly; that is, being completely unconcerned. To be sure, the call to trust and not to worry was at the heart of Jesus' teaching. But you may remember on one occasion he said to his followers, ''Now is my soul troubled.'' Jesus admitted that there is a place for positive concern, a place where worry can be constructive. We should be a bit more precise in our language and say there is a distinction between worry and concern. Worry frets about a problem, concern solves the problem. But let's use the words interchangeably to make the point.

We need to worry about situations which are not as they should be. We need to be concerned about the problem of world hunger and nuclear war. Do you remember George Bernard Shaw's famous word? ''You see things; and you say 'Why?' But I dream things that never were; and I say 'Why not?' '' Change comes when there are enough people who take that latter stand; they have a vision of the world as it should be and ask, *"Why not?"*

We are concerned not only for the world but for our cities. Why can't we have a good public school system in our city? Why can't we have decent homes for the poor? Why can't we rid our community of pornography, which poisons minds and perverts persons?

There are situations even closer to home where worry is legitimate. If your family is drifting apart, if you find yourself spending more and more money on things (thinking happiness will come, but it doesn't), if you find yourself dragging to work each day and the stress of your work becoming more intense, then you have reason for worry. I could go on and on with a catalogue of concerns that are legitimate reasons for worry.

But we need to remember this: "Worry is constructive when the focus is on what can be done about a bad situation. It is wasted energy to spend time lamenting what has already happened. 'Crying over spilled milk' leads to emotional and mental disorder; but facing the circumstances and asking what can be done about them not only changes the world, but it also builds mental and spiritual muscle. It is alright to worry if we worry in the right way, and about the right things" (Fitzgerald, p. 5).

Reflecting and Recording

On the lines below, list in a word or two the things you have worried about during the past month.

_____

_____

_____

Now look at each one and ask the question, was this *legitimate* worry? Put a check (√) by the ones you think legitimate.

※　※　※

Now look at the ones you checked. Did you seek, or are you seeking, to do anything to change that about which you have legitimately worried?

※　※　※

During the Day

Memorize this verse: "Therefore do not be anxious about tomorrow, for tomorrow will be anxious for itself. Let the day's own trouble be sufficient for the day" (Matt. 6:34). If you have difficulty memorizing, copy it on a piece of paper and carry it with you throughout the next six or seven days. Repeat it to yourself as you sit for a coffee break, or a meal, or some time when you are alone. This is Jesus' antidote for worry.

Day Two: *Security in God*

Return to the text for yesterday and read the section from Jesus' Sermon on the Mount, Matthew 6:25–33.

✳ ✳ ✳

Many years ago Dr. James Fisher, a practicing psychiatrist, wrote a very entertaining little book entitled *A Few Buttons Missing*. It was light treatment of some of his experiences in psychiatric practice. However, near the end of the book, Dr. Fisher became very serious. This is what he said.

What was needed, I felt sure, was some new and enlightened recipe for living a sane and satisfying life—a recipe compounded from all the accumulated scientific knowledge acquired through study and research. . . . I dreamed of writing a handbook that would be simple, practical, easy to understand, and easy to follow. It would tell people how to live—what thoughts and attitudes and philosophies to cultivate, and what pitfalls to avoid, in seeking mental health. I attended every symposium it was possible for me to attend, and I took notes on the wise words of my teachers and of my colleagues who were leaders in their field.

And then quite by accident, I discovered that such a work had already been completed. . . . If you were to take the sum total of all the authoritative articles ever written by the most qualified of psychologists and psychiatrists on the subject of mental hygiene—if you were to combine them, and refine them, and cleave out the excess verbage—if you were to take the whole of the meat and none of the parsley, and if you were to have these unadulterated bits of pure scientific knowledge concisely expressed by the most capable of living poets, you would have an awkward and incomplete summation of the Sermon on the Mount. And it would suffer immeasurably through comparison (Fisher and Lowell, p. 273).

Did you note that Jesus began this passage with the word *therefore*? This is a bridge word, and when you see it in scripture you need to stop and ask what it is there for. In this instance, Jesus is emphasizing that, having become a disciple, we can look to our Master for his care and trust him for our well-being. This scripture is a call to trust God as an answer to one of the most plaguing human problems with which we have to cope: worry.

Myron Augsberger, the popular Mennonite scholar and preacher, provides an insightful commentary on this passage. He says Jesus is teaching that worry is *irreverent, irrelevant,* and *irresponsible.*

> Jesus presents evidence that worry is *irreverent,* for it fails to recognize the God who gave us life and is sustaining it. Worry is *irrelevant;* it does not change things, nor does it help us in coping with problems. And worry is *irresponsible;* it burns up psychic energy without using it to apply constructive action to the problem. Jesus used the birds of the air to illustrate freedom from anxiety, the lilies of the field to illustrate freedom from status-seeking, and the grass of the field to illustrate our need to assess priorities. Interspersed with his illustrations are his admonitions. In verse 27, he says that by worry we cannot add to our span of life; we may even limit it! In verse 32, he contrasts the way of the members of the kingdoms of this world with the way of the children of the Father (Augsberger, p. 94).

Now let's take that a little slower. Why do we worry? We worry about our needs—food, clothing, housing. The way we worry about these needs is different from the way most of the people of the world worry about them. We have food, clothing, and shelter. There are people in our city who do not and millions of people around the world who do not. But we worry, nonetheless, about our jobs, our economic security, about what we will do and how we will live when we retire. Jesus says, "Look at the birds of the air: they neither sow nor reap nor gather into barns, and yet your heavenly Father feeds them. Are you not of more value than they?"

Not only about needs, we worry about our status, our relationships. How am I coming off? Am I really liked? What does John really think about me? How much time and energy do we invest in our distorted notions about status? Think of the money we spend on *status*. No where is this more bizarrely funny in the United States than in the money we spend on designer brand clothing: we pay more for a shirt with an alligator on it rather than a fox or a polo player rather than an alligator. We worry so much about status. Jesus says, "Consider the lilies of the field, how they grow; they neither toil nor spin; yet I tell you even Solomon in all his glory was not arrayed like one of these" (vv. 28–29).

Jesus then presses his point home by admonishing us to continually *assess our priorities*. Think of the way you spend your time. What do you think about? To what do you give most of your energy? Think about your priorities and listen to Jesus. "But if God so clothes the grass of the field, which today is alive and tomorrow is thrown into the oven, will he not much more clothe you, O men of little faith?" (v. 30)

What is the bottom line of Jesus' teaching? It's so simple, yet so difficult to live. *When we have found our security in God, we can trust God with our needs.* Christ is calling us to give up our limited securities for the greater security of God's grace.

The question is, "How do we do that?" How do we live out a commitment to the security of God's grace! Tomorrow we will look at practical ways to practice the security which is ours in God's grace, the security which will free us from destructive worry.

Reflecting and Recording

Look back at the list of worries you recorded yesterday. Record them here according to the category you would place them in. If they do not fit into worry about needs or status, put them in the "other" column.

NEEDS	STATUS	OTHER
_____	_____	_____
_____	_____	_____
_____	_____	_____
_____	_____	_____

My hunch is that when you made your list yesterday, you didn't give much attention to status. Having thought about that, do you have any worries you would add to either the "status" or "other" categories? Do so now. Be honest!

❋ ❋ ❋

Spend some time in prayer about your worry. What about your daily life are you not commiting to the security of God's grace?

❋ ❋ ❋

During the Day

Copy the following prayer by Reinhold Niebuhr and take it with you in your pocket or purse. Or put it in a place you will see often such as the bathroom mirror, the refrigerator door, the family bulletin board. Pray it as often as you can.

> God grant me the serenity to accept
>   the things I cannot change,
> Courage to change the things I can,
> And wisdom to know the difference.

Day Three: *Practicing the Security of God's Grace*

In the *During the Day* section yesterday, we shared the prayer from Reinhold Niebuhr. Let's begin with that prayer today.

> God grant me the serenity to accept
>   the things I cannot change,
> Courage to change the things I can,
> And wisdom to know the difference.

There are two things we should never worry about: the things we can't help and the things we can. Why worry about the things you cannot help? What good will it do? That's what Jesus is telling us: "Which of you by being anxious can add one cubit to his span of life?" (Matt. 6:27).

But what about the second category—worrying about things we can help? On Day One, we talked about *legitimate* worry. It is a mark of responsibility to be concerned about certain issues. But there comes the point when worry is irresponsible; it is wasting energy. If we can help, then we must—and now. The reason worry kills more people than work is that more people worry than work.

So the first practical way to practice the security of God's grace is not to worry about two things: what you can't help and what you can. If you can't help, you are wasting energy to worry. If you can help, then do so, and do so now. To worry and not to act when you can is irresponsible.

Now, the second practical way to practice the security that is ours in

God's grace which will free us from destructive worry is to remember that there are two days we should never worry about—yesterday and tomorrow. Yesterday is gone! You can't correct its blunders. You can't right its mistakes. You can't undo the deeds that you did. You can't take back the words you spoke. All of that has been done, and you have no control over it.

Why worry about the past? Confess its blunders to the One who can forgive them, and who does forgive, the One who promised that if we confess our sins, he is faithful and just to forgive us our sins and to cleanse us of all unrighteousness. So don't worry about yesterday.

And don't worry about tomorrow. Worry is an emotion that can never empty tomorrow of its problem, but while you worry about tomorrow you are emptying today of its strength. Tomorrow is not yet. Its promise and its potential problems are out of reach. You can do nothing about tomorrow until it has arrived. You can, however, remember what Paul said: "For God is at work in you, both to will and to work for his good purpose" (Phil. 2:13). And you can remember what Jesus said: "Seek first his kingdom and his righteousness, and all these things shall be yours as well" (Matt. 6:33).

There follows naturally a third practical way to practice the security that is ours in God's grace to free us from destructive worry. Focus always on today and do today everything you can to live fully, and trust Christ with all your needs.

Said the Robin to the Sparrow,
"I would really like to know
Why those anxious human beings
Rush around and worry so."

Said the Sparrow to the Robin,
"Friend, I think that it must be
That they have no Heavenly Father
Such as cares for you and me."
　　　　　　　　　　—Anonymous

Look at the birds of the air;
they neither sow nor reap nor gather into barns,
and yet your heavenly Father feeds them.
Are you not of more value than they?
　　　　　　　　　　—Matthew 6:26

Reflecting and Recording

List three or four big concerns of your life right now.

Consider each of these concerns by asking yourself the following questions. Can I do anything about this today? Can I begin to take some positive steps in response to this concern, steps that may be ongoing? Is this concern about a past issue that I must leave behind? Is it a future issue to which I can't respond now?

Make this list a matter of prayer as you examine each concern, making whatever confession and commitment you need to make, and seeking God's guidance and grace.

✳   ✳   ✳

During the Day

Try to move through this day without the burden of yesterday's failure or the diversion of anxiety about tomorrow.

Day Four: *The Painful Presence of Guilt*

I met him in a restaurant. We were both leaving, so we stopped on the sidewalk outside for a visit. What began as a casual exchange flowed into the sharing of deep feeling. A question about his family triggered a brief convulsion of distress and pain. He was estranged from his son. He had done everything he could, so he thought, to bring about reconciliation. But there was still the tension, the strain, the cold, formal relating without genuine warmth. The fellow told me he dreams about his son and awakens in the middle of the night and remains sleepless for hours, thinking about the painful estrangement. "And the guilt is wearing me out," he said. "Despite my efforts, I am plagued with guilt, and I can't get it out of my mind."

If we had not had that exchange at that particular time, I believe the man would have exploded emotionally somewhere during that day.

Nothing weighs more heavily upon us. Nothing drains more emotional energy. Guilt is a painful reality in our lives. In fact, there are few, if any, human emotions that are as distressing and painful as guilt. When at a peak of intensity, guilt gnaws at the conscious mind by day and invades the dreams by night.

The voice of conscience speaks from inside the human mind. It is often an accusing voice, raging at us for our mistakes, failures, and sins. This voice of conscience can be a saving one, calling us to confession and repentance, reminding us of our failures in relationships. It can also be a condemning and destructive force, tormenting us to distraction, even to mental illness. How do we cope as Christians?

There are instances of extreme guilt in which persons are so tormented with self-blame and self-hatred that they need professional medical and psychological help. Using this workbook and sharing with others who are genuinely seeking to cope as Christians will help us see the level of our need.

Parenthetically, it is the mark of Christian concern that persons share honestly and speak the truth in love. It may be a beautiful sign of Christian concern for someone to suggest that you seek professional help or for you to suggest to someone else that they may need to seek professional help from a pastor or a counselor. This should be done privately, not in a group setting. Such suggestions will be heard if trust is present and feelings of genuine concern are expressed. This is true not only in the area of guilt, but in all areas of concern with which we are dealing.

Let's begin a process which will help us get our guilt into perspective. First, clarify your feelings. Now this sounds simple, but it isn't. Our minds and consciences play tricks on us. As long as guilt remains a vague, unnamed, oppressive stirring within, we can't deal with it; so we need to be specific. Why am I having this guilty feeling? What have I done to bring it on? Clarify your feelings.

Closely akin to this is the second principle. Recognize that your guilty conscience may be rooted in an illegitimate feeling of responsibility. I'm saying that you can *blame* yourself and *drive* yourself to emotional torment by taking responsibility for what you can't control. So, as you deal with guilt, ask yourself what is bringing the guilt on, and try to determine if you have any control over it.

Three, most guilt produced by sin against, or the violation of, another can be assuaged by genuinely taking the blame and seeking forgiveness. I don't mean that reconciliation is easy. It isn't. Sometimes we seek the forgiveness of the person we have wronged and that person becomes stubborn, mean, vindictive, and will not reciprocate—will neither accept our forgiveness nor offer us his or hers. That means that we pay the price of sin. We suffer because of our wrongdoing. Our suffering is in the form of mental anguish, the pain of separation, relationships that are cold and formal until forgiveness is actualized in the relationship, and the estrangement is dissolved.

But remember this. If you are feeling guilty over a relationship that is not what it should be, nothing is going to happen to assuage that guilt until you take a step, until you take the initiative and are willing to bear responsibility, confess that responsibility, and initiate the forgiving process.

Reflecting and Recording

Locate in your mind now, bring clearly to consciousness, one matter of guilt which you are feeling deeply. Get the matter clearly in mind. To gain perspective on it, move through the clarifying process we have just considered.

✳ ✳ ✳

If the guilt is about a relationship, determine now that (if you haven't already) you will seek forgiveness from the other or offer forgiveness.

If that has already been done and the person has refused to receive or give forgiveness, pray each day that by a miracle of God's grace the person will become open to the reconciling power of forgiveness.

If the guilt is the result of your taking responsibility for what you can't control, ask God to relieve you of that illegitimate burden, and determine now that you are not going to continue to blame yourself.

Now, rest for a minute in this promise of scripture. "If we confess our sins, he is faithful and just, and will forgive our sins and cleanse us from all unrighteousness" (1 John 1:9).

During the Day

When guilt invades your thoughts today, register as clearly as possible the source of the guilt. When you have time, sometime during the day or before you sleep tonight, bring the guilt into the clarifying light of the process we have been considering.

Day Five: *Approach God's Throne, Where There Is Grace*

There are two points in our lives at which guilt operates in an extremely debilitating way. One is in our role as parents. It is not unusual for parents to take responsibility for everything wrong in and about their children, even blaming themselves for distorted, broken, brain-damaged children because of genes passed on or accident of birth.

The second point in our lives at which guilt operates in an extremely debilitating way is the conflict between what we may call the "achieved self" and the "potential self." We sometimes become devastatingly guilty because we have not achieved what we set out to achieve, or we have not become what we once envisioned becoming.

That is the way it must be when we look at ourselves. We need to keep a healthy understanding of what we have become in terms of what we have the potential of becoming. To be the best that we can be, to be all that God created us to be, "to bloom where we are planted" is as it should be. We need to remember that there are no inferior people. Each one of us is a unique, unrepeatable miracle of God. We all have our unique strengths, but we also have our weaknesses. When we utilize our strength, our weakness is minimized. When we recognize our weakness, we do not have to waste our energy or wallow in guilt about lack of talent and/or lack of achievement. We need to be *concerned* but *not guilty* when our "potential self" is not being realized.

Let's move now to the point at which I believe our inability to cope with guilt focuses. To get the point before us, consider the word of scripture.

Let us, then, do our best to receive that rest, so that no one of us will fail as they did because of their lack of faith.

The word of God is alive and active, sharper than any double-edged sword. It cuts all the way through, to where soul and spirit meet, to where joints and marrow come together. It judges the desires and thoughts of man's heart. There is nothing that can be hid from God; everything in all creation is exposed and lies open before his eyes. And it is to him that we must all give an account of ourselves.

Let us, then, hold firmly to the faith we profess. For we have a great High Priest who has gone into the very presence of God—Jesus, the Son of God. Our High Priest is not one who cannot feel sympathy for our weaknesses. On the contrary, we have a High Priest who was tempted in every way that we are, but did not sin. Let us be brave, then, and approach God's throne, where there is grace. There we will receive mercy and find grace to help us just when we need it.

—Hebrews 4:11–16, TEV

Now, let me be bold in sounding my thesis. Most of us are riddled with guilt because we do not accept the fact that at God's throne there is grace. It is a deep religious question, perhaps the deepest of all religious questions, having to do with the nature of God. Let me tell you two stories.

One of them comes from South Africa. The attention of the world is on that violent nation. Alan Paton is one of the giants of that land. In his novel, *Too Late the Phalarope,* he gives us this scene. A white police lieutenant has secretly carried on an affair with a black African woman. In South Africa that is against the law in every way. Not only is it against the civil law, but in that stern, racist society, it was an abominable sin, an unforgivable sin.

The lieutenant is confronted with the charge by his captain. The lieutenant denies the charge, but the evidence is so overwhelming that he finally confesses. The captain does what might appear to be a strange thing. He goes to visit the lieutenant's father and shares with him his son's transgression. It is a moving and tragic scene.

The father asks the captain, ''Is it true?''

The captain replies, ''I fear it is true.''

The father insists, ''Are you sure?''

The captain says, ''He confessed to me. It's true.''

Then there was silence except for the sound of the father's deep breathing. It was like the breathing of some creature in agonizing pain.

In the room observing the scene is the wife of the father (the son's mother) and the father's sister. The father turns to the sister and says, ''Bring me the Book.'' She goes to the bookcase, pulls down the heavy family Bible, takes it to the man, and sets it before him on the table. She wonders what passage he is going to read.

The fellow doesn't read any passage at all. Instead he opens the front of the book where family names had been recorded for 150 years. He takes the pen and ink and crosses out the name of his son, Pieter van Vlaanderen, not once but many times as though to completely obliterate it from the page. Without any anger or despair (at least that anybody could see), without any words, he does that dramatic task. Then he turns to the captain and very calmly asks, ''Is there anything more?'' The captain knows that this is his cue to leave the house, and he does, offering to the mother any kind of help he might be able to afford.

But the father turns abruptly to him and says, ''No one in this house will ask for help.'' So the captain leaves.

Then the father, still sitting at the table, turns to his sister and says, ''Lock the door, and bolt it, and bring me the key. The door of our house will never open again.''

That's the scene. The door is closed forever. The son can never return home. (Paraphrased. Paton, pp. 249–251).

Now, you may have leaped ahead in your mind to the story from the Bible that I would set over against that one. A father had two sons. One of those sons left home and squandered his inheritance in riotous and wasteful living. The son reduced himself to nothing—to the level of nothingness as a Jew would perceive it—the life of feeding hogs. It was the abominable sin, the disgrace of all disgraces for the family, the most terrible humiliation a father could suffer because of his son.

You know the story. The father, of course, either learns about or suspects the kind of life his son is living. His heart is broken. But he doesn't close the door of his house; in fact, he keeps it wide open. No, more than that. Not only does he keep the door wide open, but every day he wanders down the lane and looks as far as he can, hoping and praying that his son will come to himself and return home. And that happens. The father sees him at a distance, runs down to greet him, throws his arms around him, and won't even let his son make his rehearsed confession. The father embraces his son, kisses him, begins to make ready for a great celebration that includes the giving of the family ring and the killing of a fatted calf and the placing of a rich robe around his shoulder. "My son who was dead is alive; my son who was lost is found" (Luke 15:32, AP).

These two stories state the case dramatically. In our humanness, we think that when we sin, when we play havoc with our life and the lives of others, the door is closed.

The only positive thing about this way of thinking is that it says we know the seriousness of our offenses. But the truth is that the door is not closed. That's what the parable of the Prodigal Son teaches us. That is what the word from Hebrews says. "Let us be brave, then, and approach God's throne, where there is grace . . . to help us just when we need it" (Heb. 4:16, TEV).

That is the only way we will find ultimate relief for guilt. Our sin, you see, even our sin against others, is also sin against God. If we are going to deal with guilt at its root, we've got to deal with it in our relationship to God.

Reflecting and Recording

"Let us be brave, then, and approach God's throne, where there is grace. There we will receive mercy and find grace to help us just when we need it." Ponder that word for a few minutes, then write a prayer of confession, naming your feelings of guilt, confessing your sin, and claiming the mercy and grace of the living Christ.

✳ ✳ ✳

PRAYER OF CONFESSION

During the Day

One of the dynamics of forgiveness which frees us from guilt is confession. Sometimes the forgiveness of Christ is actualized in our lives by confession to another. We will deal more with this later. For now you may want to find a trusted friend with whom you can share your guilt or confess your sin. Let that person know why you are doing it—as a dynamic you are testing from this workbook adventure.

Day Six: *Fear Crackles Like a Fire in Every Life*

Did you hear the story of the 747 jetliner taxiing out onto the runway, passengers all buckled up for the takeoff? At the end of the runway, the plane stopped. A voice came over the speakers in the plane's cabin: "Good morning, ladies and gentlemen, this is your captain speaking; welcome aboard Flight 22 for London's Heathrow Airport. We will climb to a cruising altitude of 30,000 feet and will travel at an air speed of 600 miles per hour. Our flight plan will take us across Canada, Greenland, Iceland, and over the tip of Ireland. Our flying time will be about nine hours. As soon as we are airborne your flight attendants will be serving you breakfast. We'll take off . . . just as soon as I can get up the nerve!"

Anyone who is alive knows the experience of fear for fear crackles like a fire in every life. This fire is fed by the uncertainties that are a constant part of people and events.

Stop now and name four or five things, situations, relationships that come to your mind about which you are afraid. Note them in a word or sentence.

Is it any wonder that we dream about running away? We dream about some safe and lovely faraway island, where we can be quiet and secure, removed from the hectic pressures and the forces that bring fear to our lives weekly, if not daily. How do we cope as Christians? Is there a way to deal positively with our fears, and either let them serve us or overcome them if they are negative and destructive?

It is obvious that I believe not all fear is bad. Fear may be a healthy force in our life. A person who is utterly fearless is a fool! I don't want to ride in an automobile with a person who is utterly foolish.

As human beings, fear is one of our basic alarm systems. It is an instinct that leads us to fight or flight and can save us from danger and suffering.

Fear is a creative force. It has been responsible for some of humanity's greatest advances. Fear of death drives us to seek cures for cancer and other life threatening diseases. Fear of ignorance stimulates nations to take responsibility for the education of their citizenry, passing laws of basic school attendance requirements.

Fear of war in a nuclear age mobilizes us against the development of nuclear power as a weapon and sends many to jail in protest against nuclear madness.

So fear may be a positive force in our lives. What we are looking for is not utter fearlessness, but confidence over fear, the resources to control the debilitating fears that invade our lives. Do we need to name those debilitating fears?

- Fear of failure that keeps us from risking or even trying.
- Fear of inner weakness which burns like a fire within, making our life a hell of inner conflict.
- Fear that flows from our doubt about personal ability or about the faithfulness of our marriage mate, a fear which can make us impotent.

- Fear of being found out in our moral weakness or in our fears themselves, turning us into hiding persons, wearers of masks to prevent real knowing and sharing.
- Fear of death, our own or the loss of a loved one.
- Fear of retirement because of economic insecurity.
- Fear that our children will not turn out ''good,'' that we will be failures as parents.

Look back at your list of fears recorded on page 50. Do any of them fit into the fears I have just suggested?

⁂ ⁂ ⁂

The list could go on. The question is, how do we cope? How do we become confident rather than fearful? One suggestion for today: *Name your fear and face it squarely.*

President Franklin Roosevelt used to say, ''The only thing we have to fear is fear itself.'' Naming our fear and facing it does two things. First, it sometimes puts the fear in a perspective that causes it to disappear.

I remember once going for three weeks with a growth on my back that one doctor suspected might be malignant. My wife Jerry was devastated. Her fear of my death brought all sorts of other troublesome issues to the surface, including her unhealthy dependence upon me in her own faith pilgrimage. Fear also threatened to immobilize me. We were involved in travel and speaking engagements that prevented me from obtaining a definite diagnosis of the growth. Fear was my unwelcome but constant traveling companion. When the diagnosis was finally made, the burden was lifted because the truth was known—no malignancy. The fear was put in a perspective that caused it to disappear. That often happens when we face fear squarely.

The second thing that happens when we name fear and face it squarely is that we are given a kind of power over it. Just by naming it, we get a sense of courage and power to face and overcome the fear. In the naming of fear, we are forced to face it for what it is, and the fear, if not completely overcome, often diminishes to the point that we can be confident in our strength over it.

Reflecting and Recording

Go back to the list of fears you named earlier. Look at them closely. Did you really name them? Select one of those that is most oppressive. Write a paragraph on the next page about how you feel about that fear. Call it for what it is. Bring it into the open and determine to follow up until you are facing it squarely.

Read now and rest in the assurance of the Twenty-third Psalm.

The Lord is my shepherd, I shall not want;
  he makes me lie down in green pastures.
He leads me beside still waters;
  he restores my soul.
He leads me in paths of righteousness
  for his name's sake.

Even though I walk through the valley
  of the shadow of death,
  I fear no evil;
for thou art with me;
  thy rod and thy staff,
  they comfort me.

Thou preparest a table before me
  in the presence of my enemies;
thou anointest my head with oil,
  my cup overflows.
Surely goodness and mercy shall follow me
  all the days of my life;
and I shall dwell in the house of the Lord
  for ever.

One line in the Psalm addresses our fears in a special way: "Thou preparest a table before me in the presence of my enemies" (v. 5). That speaks of the Lord's protection. With that protection, we need not fear.

During the Day

Do you know the Twenty-third Psalm by heart? If not, start work on memorizing it. Repeat as much of the psalm as you know throughout the day, especially that one affirmation: ''Thou preparest a table before me in the presence of my enemies.'' When fear invades your life, call that truth to mind.

Day Seven: *Our God Protects Us*

''If fear were abolished from modern life, the work of psychotherapists would be nearly gone.'' That is the word of an eminent psychiatrist, Dr. J. A. Hadfield (Moyes, p. 21).

Dr. Frank Mayfield, one of the United States' outstanding neurosurgeons, who operates upon the nerves of cancer patients to relieve their pain, has come to the following conclusion:

> Most of the pain that patients with cancer experience emanates from emotional stimuli, arising from anxiety and fear, a fear of the unknown, a fear of death. I am convinced that much of it would be alleviated if people understood their condition and had some religious faith. I have observed that when a cancer patient turns to his religion, he experiences surprising relief from anxiety, and fear, and pain! (Moyes, p. 23).

This speaks of naming and squarely facing our fear, but it also speaks of another significant tool for coping with fear: *trusting the protecting power of God*.

As I write this, I feel a wrenching need to ''practice what I preach.'' My daughter just called and informed me that our only grandson, Nathan, has a problem called nystagmus. His eyes won't stay steady or focused.

Nathan is four months old. There was a problem at his birth and we have had a gnawing fear that it might have caused some defects. Nothing has indicated anything but normal growth and development. He is a happy, healthy baby—but now this. He will see a pediatric ophthalmologist, but not for three weeks. The problem could be muscular, neurological, or even an inner ear problem.

My daughter expressed the natural concern of a mother, and fear is there. But she urges me (as I'm sure she tries to convince herself) that while this is serious, we must keep it in perspective. One sure sign of hope is that Nathan has not been otherwise affected; another is that you never see adults with this type of nystagmus, so it obviously can be corrected or outgrown.

Fear is present, and we need to cope during these next three weeks as we await the diagnosis of the pediatric ophthalmologist. The Psalms are full of other affirmations like the beloved and well-known Twenty-third Psalm.

Thou, O Lord, art a shield about me,
my glory, and the lifter of my head.
—Psalm 3:3

The Lord is a stronghold for the oppressed,
a stronghold in times of trouble.
—Psalm 9:9

I love thee, O Lord, my strength,
The Lord is my rock, and my fortress, and my deliverer,
my God, my rock, in whom I take refuge,
my shield, and the horn of my salvation, my stronghold.
—Psalm 18:1–2

These psalms speak of trust and commitment. The Lord will protect us in the midst of circumstances and forces that would lead us astray and take us far from God's righteous path.

Gordon Moyes, the popular preacher and writer in Sydney, Australia, tells of Marjorie Lawrence's conquest of fear by trust in God. She was a great Australian opera singer who, at the height of her operatic career in 1941, became paralyzed with polio that crippled her. She couldn't stand or move or sing. Her case seemed hopeless.

One night Marjorie Lawrence asked her husband, "What will I do, Tom?" He replied, "Everybody does seem to think your case is hopeless, but there is God. Let us turn to him and have faith. I know he will help."

Though overwhelmed with fears of suffering and invalidism, they faced these fears, and read the Psalms. Marjorie Lawrence wrote:

There were parts of scripture written especially for me, a divine prescription for my ailing spirit: "The Lord is my strength and song, and has become my salvation; The Lord is my light and my salvation; whom shall I fear? The Lord is the strength of my life; of whom shall I be afraid?"

Humbly then, with faith in our hearts, my husband and I prayed, prayed not so much that I should be cured but that we should be given courage and hope to continue our lives, to bear our crosses with patience and fortitude. From the day we acknowledged God's part in the scheme of things and turned to him, there was a miraculous change in my mental outlook. Faith and prayer cast out my fears, and the will to fight, the will to win, was restored to me!

"Faith and prayer cast out my fears!" Gordon Moyes reported that with fear removed, new hope strengthened Marjorie Lawrence's resolve to recover and to sing again. By constant, painful exercising she fought her way back to a new career singing around the world.

"In the dark days of World War II, Marjorie Lawrence was wheeled through the camps singing to the troops. They recognized her courage, her fortitude and her hope. Her fearlessness encouraged them in a way few others ever could'' (Moyes, pp. 27–28).

Reflecting and Recording

One reason our fear is often so great is that we hide it from others. Secret fears, deep within us, can poison our physical system as well as our emotional life. I'm told by doctors that our adrenal glands secrete epinephrine into our bodies when stimulated by fear. This is a part of God's miraculous creation of our bodies. This powerful secretion, triggered by fear, provides the extra energy we need to run faster than we ever thought we could when faced by danger or to lift impossible loads under which another may be trapped.

But too much epinephrine may poison the system; thus deep and secret fears may bring about physical problems such as nausea, fainting, heart palpitations, trembling, even convulsions. For this reason, people who are free from guilt and have fear eliminated from their lives may have a sense of inner peace which helps them recover more rapidly from ailments than fearful patients.

The point is that we flirt with physical as well as emotional danger when we hide our fears, when we keep them buried within. Are you flirting with such danger? Is there some deep secret fear you need to share with a trusted friend? Examine your life now.

❊　❊　❊

Do you have a close friend or a pastor with whom you need to share your fear? Find a time to do so soon.

During the Day

The classic verse of scripture offering an antidote for fear is 1 John 4:18: "There is no fear in love, but perfect love casts out fear." Today, and in the days ahead, work to love perfectly in those situations where there is fear. Claim the love of Christ which is perfect in relation to you—unlimited and unconditional. Christ's love for you, when claimed, replaces fear with peace.

Group Meeting for Week Two

Introduction

Participation in a group such as this is a covenant relationship. You will profit most as you keep the daily discipline of the thirty-minute period and as you faithfully attend these weekly meetings. Do not feel guilty if you have to miss a day in the workbook or be discouraged if you are not able to give the full thirty minutes in daily discipline. Don't hesitate sharing that with the group. We may learn something about ourselves as we share. We may discover, for instance, that we are unconsciously afraid of dealing with the content of a particular day because of what is required and what it reveals about us. Be patient with yourself and always be open to what God may be seeking to teach you.

Our growth, in part, hinges upon our group participation, so share as openly and honestly as you can. Listen to what persons are saying. Sometimes there is meaning beyond the surface of their words which you may pick up if you are really attentive.

Being a sensitive participant in this fashion is crucial. Responding immediately to the feelings we pick up is also crucial. Sometimes it is important for the group to focus its entire attention upon a particular individual. If some need or concern is expressed, it may be appropriate for the leader to ask the group to enter into a brief period of special prayer for the persons or concerns revealed. Participants should not always depend upon the leader for this kind of sensitivity, for the leader may miss it. Even if you aren't the leader, don't hesitate to ask the group to join you in special prayer. This praying may be silent, or some person may wish to lead the group in prayer.

Remember, you have a contribution to make to the group. What you consider trivial or unimportant may be just what another person needs to hear. We are not seeking to be profound but simply to share our experience.

Sharing Together

Note: It will not be possible in this time frame to use all these suggestions. The leader should select what will be most beneficial to the group. It is important that the leader be thoroughly familiar with these suggestions in order to move through them *selectively* according to the direction in which the group is moving and according to the time available. The leader should plan ahead, but do not hesitate to change your plan according to the nature of the sharing taking place and the needs that emerge.

1. Open your time together with the leader offering a brief prayer of thanksgiving for the opportunity of sharing with the group and petitions for openness in sharing and loving response to each other.

2. Let each person share the most meaningful day in this week's workbook adventure.

3. Now share the most difficult day and tell why it was difficult.

4. Spend a few minutes talking about *legitimate* and *illegitimate* worry. When is worry constructive?

5. Ask the group to focus on the matters about which they worry. Does this worry have to do with needs, status, or some other category? Persons may want to review their Reflecting and Recording on Day Two.

6. Ask if any person can share some helpful revelation about how they saw their concerns after examining them in light of being able to do something about them as suggested in Reflecting and Recording on Day Three.

7. Discuss the issue of guilt that comes from taking illegitimate responsibility. Does anyone have a personal witness to this?

8. Grace is the keynote of the gospel. Why do we have such difficulty accepting it?

9. Can someone share an experience of forgiveness and freedom from guilt by confession?

Praying Together

As stated last week, the effectiveness of this group and the quality of relationship will be enhanced by a commitment to pray for each other by name each day. If you have pictures of each other, as requested last week, put these pictures face down on a table and let each person select a picture. This person will be the focus of special prayer for the week. Bring the photos back next week, shuffle them and draw again. Continue this throughout your pilgrimage together. Looking at a person's picture as you pray for that person will add meaning. Having the picture will also remind you that you are to give special prayer attention to this person during the week.

1. Praying corporately each week is a special ministry. Take some time now for a period of verbal prayer, allowing each person to mention any special needs he or she wishes to share with the entire group.

A good pattern is to ask for a period of prayer after each need is mentioned. There may be silent prayer by the entire group, or someone may offer a brief two-or-three-sentence verbal prayer.

2. Close your time by praying together the great prayer of the church, "Our Father." As you pray this prayer, remember that you are linking yourselves with all Christians of all time in universal intercession.

Words of Encouragement

As you begin this third week of your journey, here are some thoughts to keep in mind.

Discipline is an important dimension of life. Discipline is not slavish rigidity but an ordering of life that enables you to control your circumstances rather than being controlled by them. For most people, a designated time of prayer is essential for building a life of prayer.

If you have not yet established a regular time to use this workbook and as your prayer time, try to find the right time for you this week. Experiment: in the morning, after work, during the lunch hour, before retiring. Find time that seems best for you.

If you discover that you can't cover all the workbook material and exercises given for a day, don't berate yourself. Get what you can out of what you do. There is no point in rushing over three or four steps or principles if you cannot think deeply. Consider them seriously one by one, and move only as far as you can.

Intellectual assent to a great principle or possibility is important, but it does us little good until we act upon it—until we say yes in our minds, and live it out in relationships.

Don't hesitate to make decisions and resolves, but don't condemn yourself if you fail. God is patient and wants us to be patient with ourselves.

Stress and Distress

Day One: *In the Lion's Den*

The king commanded, and Daniel was brought and cast into the den of lions. The king said to Daniel, "May your God, whom you serve continually, deliver you!" And a stone was brought and laid upon the mouth of the den, and the king sealed it with his own signet and with the signet of his lords, that nothing might be changed concerning Daniel. Then the king went to his palace, and spent the night fasting; no diversions were brought to him, and sleep fled from him.

Then, at break of day, the king arose and went in haste to the den of the lions. When he came near to the den where Daniel was, he cried out in a tone of anguish and said to Daniel, "O Daniel, servant of the living God, has your God, whom you serve continually, been able to deliver you from the lions?" Then Daniel said to the king, "O king, live for ever! My God sent his angel and shut the lions' mouths, and they have not hurt me, because I was found blameless before him; and also before you, O king, I have done no wrong." Then the king was exceedingly glad, and commanded that Daniel be taken up out of the den. So Daniel was taken up out of the den, and no kind of hurt was found upon him, because he had trusted in his God.

—Daniel 6:16–23

I don't know when it began, but the symbol has been a pervasive one for a long time—the lion's den. It is a symbol for the conflictual dimensions of life. "They threw him to the lions," we say of those who cruelly thrust an innocent, unsuspecting person into the most difficult of all situations.

"The lion's den" is the place where our testing comes, where we struggle to keep our integrity, where we wage the fiery battle with

61

ourselves as well as with others and/or forces outside ourselves. It may be the arena where we fight for our very life.

It is an expansive image, but I want to use it in a focused way for perhaps the most common problem we face today—the problem of stress and distress. Psychologists and psychiatrists say this is one of the most pervasive and difficult struggles in contemporary society.

The business world is giving stress priority attention because it is playing havoc with performance and productivity. Medical doctors are telling us that much of the illness they are treating these days is related to stress. In many instances, stress is the cause of the problem. But if not the cause, in almost all instances, the relief of stress must be part of the cure. We can't be healthy unless we learn to live with stress.

So that's the symbol we want to pursue, *living in the lion's den,* as we continue our look at coping as Christians. I doubt if the image goes back to the Old Testament prophet Daniel, but it might. Rehearse that story, a part of which is recorded above. King Darius loved and respected Daniel, had made him one of three presidents who presided over the affairs of the kingdom. Daniel had become the most distinguished of all. Jealousy set in, and some of the lesser officials in King Darius's government tricked the king into setting up rules for worship, rules that required people to worship no other but the king for at least thirty days. Daniel was caught in the trap; and, much to the grief and despair of King Darius, he was thrown into the lions' den. All night long the king fasted and prayed. When he went to the den the next morning, the lions' mouths had been stopped, and not the least bit of harm had been done to Daniel.

That's the picture—living in the lions' den. The psalmist cried, "Save me from the mouth of the lion" (Psalm 22:21). So that image has been with us for a long time. Just recently I read an article in a business magazine which referred to top management's place of work and network of relationships as *the lion's den!*

We don't need to further analyze the image, because it communicates well enough. It is the image of conflict and uneasiness, the image of feeling that we're dealing with something that is beyond our control, the image of fear and insecurity. Let's see it as that, the image for stress in which we are all caught to some degree, and many of us are desperately caught. The psalmist knew the feeling, though he lived in a time far different from ours. He cried out, "Preserve me, O God, for in thee I take refuge" (Psalm 16:1). We will look more intently at Psalm 16 on Day Five because the images of stress are implicit there. But more, living with and overcoming stress is there. As a scripture lesson today, look at verses 9 and 10:

> Therefore my heart is glad, and my soul rejoices;
> my body also dwells secure.

For thou does not give me up to Sheol [hell]
or let thy godly one see the Pit.

One of the unique things about stress is the intimate connection between body and soul, the physical and the emotional; you get that connection in verse 9: ''Therefore my heart is glad, and my soul rejoices; my body also dwells secure.'' Stress is brought about by conflict between our inner and outer life, by the fatigue of our body that can no longer respond to the leadings of our heart. Stress is also brought about by guilt that brings fear, the fear that the psalmist is talking about when he affirms that God will not give us up to hell or let the godly one see the Pit. Those are images of death, punishment, and hell, all having to do with guilt and fear, thus with stress.

We cannot do an exhaustive study of stress, or examine it as fully as the reader might wish, in a few days of attention in this workbook. As with all these issues we are seeking to cope with as Christians, we can only provide some guideposts, define some directions, and pray that it will be enough to get us going in a deliberate fashion. So I am going to lay out a pathway of suggestions for coping with stress and distress.

First, acknowledge stress. I mean by that, acknowledge the fact that stress is such a part of life that we dare not ignore it or play hide and seek with it. As we acknowledge stress, we recognize that it is normal, even necessary, and that it can be a positive force in our lives, giving us the creative impetus we need for great living. It is true that some folks work better under pressure. So, a distinction needs to be made between normal, beneficial stress and harmful, destructive stress—which really becomes distress.

Stress becomes distress when there is too much input for us to deal with, when there are too many demands made of us. Those demands may be either of a physical or mental nature.

Lloyd Ogilvie has written a marvelous book which he titled, *Making Stress Work for You*. He began his study of stress with a definition of the word, because the word has become a catchall synonym for pace, pressure, and problems of life. ''We talk about being under stress, facing stressful situations, and dealing with stress-producing people. We have a general understanding of what causes stress, but too little knowledge with how to live with it.''

Ogilvie discovered that the word for stress in Latin is *strictus,* ''to be drawn tight.'' In old French, it is *estresse,* meaning narrowness or tightness. In English, a clear definition of stress is complicated by its many different meanings. However, in the world of physics and mechanics, it is used both for the forces which cause external pressure and for the internal strength to balance that pressure.

In the parlance of physics, for example, stress is a technical term for the measurement of weight strain on materials. On the other hand, in mechanics, the word *stress* is used for the internal strength of a metal to withstand an imposed weight-load. And it is interesting to note that stress capacity on metals is measured by what is called *yield-point* or *failure-point*. Yield point is the point at which the stress on the material actually makes it stronger; the failure-point is the point at which the strain exceeds the load bearing capacity of the material. I believe the same is true of human beings. External stress can strengthen our internal coping system, but extreme stress will bring us to failure or breaking point (Ogilvie, pp. 25–26).

Reflecting and Recording

Do you feel under stress now? If so, describe what is happening and what you are feeling.

At what time during the past three months have you felt the most stress? Make enough notes here to recapture the circumstances and feelings of that experience.

Tomorrow we will look at common causes of stress and whether they are connected with what you have just acknowledged. For now, remember that the Lord can deliver us from the lion's den. Recall Paul's word, ''We are afflicted in every way, but not crushed; perplexed, but not driven to despair'' (2 Cor. 4:8).

During the Day

Stress illustrates as much as any of our problems the connection between body and soul. When you feel your chest tighten or a knot form in your stomach or a flush of heat rush to your face when you are about to tackle some task, breathe deeply, try to relax, speak to your body, urging it to be calm. Don't act quickly; try to buy some time. (Everything doesn't have to be accomplished this hour!) Speak to your inner self by calling to mind that your body is the temple of the Holy Spirit. The Holy Spirit is the indwelling Christ. Hear the indwelling Christ speak peace to you. ''Peace I leave with you, my peace I give to you.''

Day Two: *Common Causes of Stress*

We are acknowledging stress as the beginning point of coping with it. A part of the acknowledging process is to keep in mind the common causes of stress. Let's look at some of those. First of all, change or crisis brings stress.

Some years ago, T. H. Holmes and R. H. Rahe developed what they called the Social Readjustment Rating Scale (Holmes, pp. 213–218). The study rated the impact of various upsetting life experiences in creating crippling stress and pressure. These various upsetting experiences were given a stress rating because it was discovered that the greater risk of illness came from the greater number of units of stress a person was experiencing. For example, with 200 to 299 stress units in a given year, your probability of suffering some form of illness within the next year is 50 percent. If it is 300 or more stress units, it jumps to 79 percent. The leading stress conditions and the number of points assigned to them were:

1. Death of a spouse—100 stress units
2. Divorce—73
3. Marital separation—65
4. Detention in jail or other institution—63
5. Death of a close family member—63
6. Major personal injury or illness—53
7. Marriage—50
8. Being fired at work—47
9. Marital reconciliation—45
10. Retirement from work—45

And on it went, listing major changes in health or behavior of a family member, major changes in our financial state, death of a close friend, critical changes in working hours or conditions, changes in residence or changes in schools.

All of these things play significant roles in bringing upon us the kind of stress that weakens our resistance and sets the stage for us to become a victim of some major physical or emotional illness. There are those who are saying that stress kills more of us than all other diseases combined. So we need to remember that *change* and *crisis* bring stress.

But there are other causes of stress that we need to acknowledge. There is the stress that comes from the pressure to *perform*. This begins very early. We put pressure on our children to perform academically as well as athletically—to be the best in their class, to be popular at school, to get into the best college, to select a profession of our choosing rather than allowing them to choose their own way and find that for which they are gifted. It begins very early and it continues throughout life. In our jobs, there is the pressure to perform. In our social relationships, there are all the expectations that are placed upon us. This pressure to perform builds stress within us.

Then there is the *pressure that comes from having our wants denied*. That is really the cause of anger: when we want something or expect something and don't get it, we become angry. Anger is one of the greatest sources, or maybe I should say one of the greatest expressions, of stress.

Another cause of stress is *denying our feelings*. Many of us become walking time bombs. We have deep feelings that we keep repressing. Some of these feelings are positive, some are negative. It doesn't matter whether they are positive or negative, the fact that we deny our feelings by repressing them creates stress. Although we are often not conscious of this stress, we cannot evade its devastating effects upon our lives.

What we feel inside, the deepest urges and loves and desires and longings of our life, must somehow find expression. If these feelings don't find expression, they create a kind of stress that is explosive, that eventually expresses itself in both physical and emotional illness. So this is the beginning of coping. Acknowledge stress, be familiar with its causes, and try to stay in touch with that which is bringing stress to your life.

Reflecting and Recording

Look back at the stress you described yesterday. Did it have anything to do with the ten major causes of stress mentioned above?

✳ ✳ ✳

Write three or four sentences about stress you may have felt in the following areas:

Pressure to perform

Having wants denied

Denying feelings

All these causes of stress can be brought under the lordship of Christ; that is, the indwelling Christ can be so alive in us that our stress level can be moderated and controlled. To abide in Christ is to receive his love and forgiveness. Also, abiding in Christ means inviting him to abide in us as a transforming power, which enables us to affirm ourselves but also to claim his power.

We do not have to be victims of that which would bring stress nor do we have to give in to the fears, anxieties, and insecurities of life. There is a source of strength beyond our own limited strength. The most effective antidote for stress is the cultivation of our awareness of the indwelling Christ. As Christians, Christ lives in us. That's what being Christian is.

Think about it. Would any of the stress you listed above have been diminished had you affirmed your awareness of the indwelling Christ?

✳   ✳   ✳

During the Day

Here are two verses of scripture that tell us who we are as Christians.

From now on, therefore, we regard no one from a human point of view; even though we once regarded Christ from a human point of view, we regard him thus no longer. Therefore, if any one is in Christ, he is a new creation, the old has passed away, behold, the new has come.
—2 Corinthians 5:16–17

Memorize verse 17. "If any one is in Christ, he is a new creation, the old has passed away, behold, the new has come." Repeat that verse often to yourself today and in the days ahead.

Day Three: *Admit Limitations*

A second suggestion for coping with stress is to admit limitations. As I mentioned earlier, stress is brought about by conflict between our inner and outer life, by the fatigue of our body that can no longer respond to the leading of our heart. It also has to do with guilt that comes when we have not done what we felt we should have done, or the fear that we will not be able to perform in the way that is expected of us or according to the expectations we place on ourselves.

We can nip stress in the bud if we will assess our own situation and admit limitations in the very beginning. We are not super men and women.

One illustration will make the point. Early last spring, I was up to my neck. I was about to go under. Stress was mounting. As I looked ahead on my calendar, what faced me was overwhelming. At least a year earlier, I had accepted some invitations that were challenging and exciting. I was to provide leadership for clergy in some spiritual renewal events at conference-wide levels and leadership in a national clergy-laity event. I am concerned about the United Methodist Church across this land, and I feel that I must give some time and energy in seeking the renewal of our church.

I had not accepted too many invitations. I was not planning to be away from my own congregation very much, and we were moving into the less busy summer season. So it wasn't that the schedule was too heavy when I put those invitations on my calendar. But other things began to pile up, things I had not reckoned with before—not all of them negative. The celebration of the fiftieth wedding anniversary of Jerry's parents and the sixtieth anniversary of my parents were both ahead. Some other personal and family concerns demanded my energy. It all looked like too much for any human being to deal with.

I had never done this before in a deliberate fashion. I looked ahead as far as I could and saw those things I could cancel without limiting the accomplishment of the task too much; and I cancelled my involvement in two major events.

Some of you can imagine the load that was lifted. It was as though a dark cloud had parted and the sun had begun to shine. It was a very simple thing, but it began at a very profound decision-making point, a decision that was very difficult for me to make. I'm a perfectionist. I'm a workaholic. I have this almost neurotic need not to let people down. So it was not an easy thing for me to dial those numbers and cancel those engagements; it was a very difficult thing. But when I did it, it was as though a heavy cloak had been taken off of me on a hot day and fresh air began to cool my skin. It was as though I was getting an internal massage that took the tension out of my inner being, very much like a massage takes the tension out of our physical bodies.

It was then that I internalized and made my own what I had intellectually claimed before, and that is this: EVERY NEED IS NOT A CALL. There is no possible way that we can serve every need about which we know. And every need that confronts us is not a call of God upon our life. To deal with stress we must admit *limitations*.

In Paul's Letter to the Philippians, there is this marvelous line: "I have learned, in whatever state I am, to be content" (Phil. 4:11). Later in the same passage there is an even more dramatic affirmation which we often quote. "I can do all things in him [Christ] who strengthens me" (4:13).

We usually forget the verse between those landmark ones: "I know how to be abased, and I know how to abound; in any and all circumstances I have learned the secret of facing plenty and hunger, abundance and want" (Phil. 4:12).

Paul was the giant he was because he was willing to admit limitations. Even Jesus had to find those times alone, to get away from the press of his ministry to center himself prayerfully in God. So must we, if we would cope with stress.

Reflecting and Recording

Look at your involvement pattern for the past month. Have there been stress points? Could these have been averted had you been willing to admit limitations? Think about that for a few minutes.

✳ ✳ ✳

In his book *Future Shock,* Alvin Toffler explains that we humans are highly adaptable to change, but not infinitely adaptable. In the transitional periods of our life which involve sudden and dramatic changes, which we considered yesterday, we greatly need what Toffler calls "stability zones." It is essential to our mental, physical, and spiritual stability to maintain routines, to have "stability zones" which we do not overtax by refusing to admit limitations.

Our home and our circle of friends is the best illustration of a "stability zone." Persons who lose a spouse run a huge risk in relocating their residence early after the death of their loved one. Most counselors agree that the spouse left alone should not make a decision about moving, except under very unusual circumstances, until at least a year is past. Our home and our friends who are *nearby* provide a "stability zone" for us as we adjust to our loss and set the course of our *new* life.

One of the reasons losing a job against our will and having to move to another city for employment is often traumatic is that we give up two "stability zones" at the same time. If we take a new job *on our own,* we have deliberately chosen to move and we depend upon our family or some other network of people to be our "stability zone." Our satisfaction from the new job helps to make up for the loss of a previous "stability zone."

We need to admit our limitations in order to retain, plan for, and/or cultivate "stability zones." Reflect a few minutes about whether you are protecting and enhancing your "stability zones."

✳ ✳ ✳

During the Day

Examine every call that comes to you today in terms of your limitations and your "stability zones."

Day Four: *Assert Your Will*

Closely akin to admitting limitations, which we talked about yesterday, is a third direction in our pathway of suggestions for coping with stress: *assert your will.*

When Paul was making his case to the Corinthians in his second letter, he wanted to make sure that they knew he was centered in his ministry and in his concern for them. He argued from the point of asserting one's will.

> Was I vacillating when I wanted to do this? Do I make my plans like a worldly man, ready to say Yes and No at once? As surely as God is faithful, our word to you has not been Yes and No. For the Son of God, Jesus Christ, whom we preached among you, Silvanus and Timothy and I, was not Yes and No; but in him it is always Yes. For all the promises of God find their Yes in him. That is why we utter the Amen through him, to the glory of God. But it is God who establishes us with you in Christ, and has commissioned us; he has put his seal upon us and given us his Spirit in our hearts as a guarantee.
>
> —2 Corinthians 1:17–22

Jesus spoke a similar word, though in the context of swearing. "Let what you say be simply 'Yes' or 'No'" (Matt. 5:37).

By asserting your will, I am not talking about competition or ego battles, nor am I talking about the neurotic need of too many of us to have our own way. I am not talking about the kind of stance which equates self-will with God's will (that arrogant position which parallels the position of the umpire: "It's not a strike or a ball until I call it."). I am talking about taking control of our lives. So much of the stress we experience comes from our inability or unwillingness to take control, to make decisions, to be willing to act and to take responsibility for our actions.

One illustration will make the point. A husband and wife were torn to pieces by family pressures. The mother of the wife controlled the whole family. Her tool was love. Does that surprise you? She gave herself unselfishly, so it seemed, for every member of the family. She was always giving. But the giving always had a hook, usually very subtle, and for years unrecognized.

The truth is her love was perverted. It was a selfish love. She did for others in order to bind them to her, to always have them around. Really, in her loving, she controlled the whole family network. When John, the husband, received an invitation to move to another city in what was a very exciting professional advancement, his mother-in-law literally went to pieces. The family gave in to her selfish control. After months of turmoil and anguish, John refused the invitation.

I doubt if John has had a happy day since. He hates his mother-in-law. He resents his wife for not supporting him more. He is bored with his work. And his hatred, resentment, and boredom make him an inadequate father at best. I believe John is a walking time bomb; he is a candidate for a heart attack and is already becoming dependent on alcohol. It would be different if John had asserted his will and taken control of his life.

Remember what we said about the image in the lion's den. We are in the lion's den when we feel we're dealing with something beyond our control, when we deny feelings or have our own wants denied.

Being in control is often a matter of our own will. A major cause of stress is unresolved guilt, especially the guilt that comes from broken relationships. We can do something about that. We can take control by initiating the forgiving relationship.

We can also lessen the stress that comes from pressure to perform, whether in our jobs or in our interpersonal relationships, if we will take control—run our job rather than allowing it to run us, admit our limitations and be willing to become vulnerable. It is amazing how others will identify with and support us when they realize that we're not giants, and we don't see ourselves as giants.

Reflecting and Recording

Do you feel that you are dealing with something beyond your control? Describe that something in a few sentences.

Is there any way you can assert your will in that situation, to gain some control, not necessarily over the situation but over your way of relating to it? Think about it. How can you assert your will?

✳   ✳   ✳

Are you experiencing stress because of a broken or strained relationship? Can you assert your will and take control by initiating forgiveness and reconciliation?

✳   ✳   ✳

During the Day

As you approach a stressful task or relationship, or are in the midst of a stressful situation or problem, take control. Assert your will by taking a break, just a few minutes, to acknowledge the indwelling Christ. Picture the calming presence of Jesus as a light illumining your surroundings, flowing into all parts of your body. You are wrapped in light. Breathe deeply but gently, relax your muscles, and acknowledge all your feelings. Claim those feelings in the presence of Christ, then release them to Christ. As you move back into your situation or relationship, confront your potentially stressful problem with the confidence that Christ is in you and that he will continue to relieve your tension and stress and give you peace.

Day Five: *Allow God to Be God*

Acknowledge your stress.

Admit your limitation.

Assert your will.

These are the three directions we have considered thus far on our pathway of suggestions for coping with stress. Now the fourth: *Allow God to be God.*

On Day One of this week, I introduced Psalm 16. The images of stress, as well as living with and overcoming stress, are in this psalm.

Preserve me, O God, for in thee
  I take refuge.
  I say to the Lord, "Thou art my Lord;
  I have no good apart from thee."
As for the saints in the land, they are the noble,
  in whom is all my delight.

Those who choose another god multiply their sorrows;
  their libations of blood I will not pour out
  or take their names upon my lips.

> The Lord is my chosen portion and my cup;
>   thou holdest my lot.
> The lines have fallen for me in pleasant places;
>   yea, I have a goodly heritage.
>
> I bless the Lord who gives me counsel;
>   in the night also my heart instructs me.
> I keep the Lord always before me;
>   because he is at my right hand, I shall not be moved.
>
> Therefore my heart is glad, and my soul rejoices;
>   my body also dwells secure.
> For thou dost not give me up to Sheol,
>   or let thy godly one see the Pit.
>
> Thou dost show me the path of life;
>   in the presence there is fullness of joy,
>   in thy right hand are pleasures for evermore.
>
> —Psalm 16

"Preserve me, O God." The psalmist is in desperate need. Whatever is going on in his life, he needs help beyond himself. "In thee I take refuge."

We said earlier that one of the unique things about stress is the intimate connection between soul and body. The psalmist affirms the relief of body and soul he has received from the Lord. "Therefore my heart is glad, and my soul rejoices; my body also dwells secure" (v. 9). Stress is brought about by conflict between our inner and outer life, by the fatigue of our body that can no longer respond to the leadings of our heart. Also, stress comes from guilt which produces fear. Deliverance from this fear is what the psalmist expresses in verse 10: "Thou dost not give me up to Sheol (death, hell)."

There is a marvelous image in verse 7: "I bless the Lord who gives me counsel; in the night also my heart instructs me." It is the image of *resting in the Lord*. The physical, mental, emotional, and spiritual energy demanded by stressful situations expands in geometric proportions over that demanded by otherwise normal living. For the Christian there is a rest that far exceeds the physical rest that is basic to all. *Rest in the Lord:* "In the night also my heart instructs me." It is the image of "heart power," the love of the indwelling Christ, renewing our minds and bodies.

We are limited. We can't go it on our own; our resources are never adequate. But when we allow God to be God, when we link ourselves to God, when the Lord becomes our portion, our cup, when we allow God to hold our lot—then God will give us counsel, and in the nights of our lion's den, God will instruct us.

There is a form of prayer that will open us to God, providing the healing, renewing, energizing power we need for living with stress. It is called *soaking prayer* and can be especially meaningful as we prepare for sleep (that doesn't always provide rest) during a stressful time. Flora Wuellner has described the soaking prayer well.

> I personally use the image of light, but some people prefer the images of water, wind, color, healing hands, wings, and so on. In this prayer, we do not ask for anything special. We just rest, let go, breathe in, and soak up the healing light of God which embraces us. We may not feel anything special; nevertheless it is a profoundly physical form of prayer in which every cell and organ of our bodies is washed, filled, and renewed in the healing light of God's love. Some people do feel warmth, waves of energy, a tingling sensation. Others have no such physical reactions. But the action of the light is a reality whether or not we immediately register it. We do not feel the ultraviolet rays of the sun, but they pervade us and affect our bodies whenever we go out into the daylight. Similarly, when we deliberately open ourselves to the healing presence of God, the deep action of divine love flows into every part of our lives. In this prayer we rest in it, breathe it, and allow it to work its transforming renewal within us. If thoughts wander, don't worry. Let them play like children in the sun (Wuellner, p. 21).

Amazingly, when we go to sleep in this fashion, even if we don't complete the prayer process before we are asleep, God ministers to us, "gives [us] counsel." And in the night while we are sleeping, our hearts (which are now in tune, in harmony with the heart of God) instruct us.

Reflecting and Recording

Take time now to practice soaking prayer. Go back and read Psalm 16. Now sit or lie in a relaxed position, and give thanks to God that "underneath are the everlasting arms" (Deut. 33:27). Put this time of prayer under Christ's spirit. Breathe gently and slowly, letting your hands remain open in a relaxed way. Image a cloud of light forming around your body. (Don't expect to see this light with physical eyes. Very few people do. But by your inward imaging, you are claiming the healing light of God that is always offered to you.) Perhaps you may image the light strong and intense or perhaps gently luminous. Perhaps it may seem to have a restful or energizing color.

Rest, and gently breathe in this surrounding light. Picture it flowing through the top of your head, slowly flowing through your tight facial muscles, relaxing them, especially around your eyes and jaw. Picture it now as a river of light quietly flowing through your whole body, calming, relaxing, releasing every part. Think of every slow, light breath as if breathing the breath of life which God breathes into every living being. If you wish, repeat from the psalm, "For with thee is the fountain of life; in thy light do we see light" (Psalm 36:9).

"If the light image is not right for you, think of God's healing water flowing around your body or of a gentle wind blowing through you. These are also biblical symbols" (Wuellner, p. 22).

During the Day

Verse 8 of Psalm 16 says, "I keep the Lord always before me; because he is at my right hand, I shall not be moved." Consciously seek to do that today. Practice doing it by brief moments of soaking prayer: Simply get still. By an act of the will, deliberately put yourself in Christ's presence. As much as possible, empty your mind of any other concern or thought, and be present to Christ. One symbolic act that may help is to picture yourself in a darkened room as you close your eyes. Keep them closed to symbolically shut out your surroundings. Imagine yourself putting your hand on a rheostat light switch, gradually turning up the light until the whole room is illumined. Experience that light as the light of Christ enfolding you. However brief a time it is, you are practicing keeping "the Lord always before me."

Day Six: *Choosing Another God*

Go back to yesterday's discussion and read Psalm 16.

✳   ✳   ✳

Let's begin by focusing on a portion of verse 4: "Those who choose another god multiply their sorrows." We are still focusing on the fourth direction on our pathway of suggestions for coping with stress: Allow God to be God.

When we allow stress to control our lives, we are choosing another god. I express that dogmatically to get your full attention. We do not have to be victims of stress. God has promised to deliver us.

Here is a dramatic story of a young paraplegic girl allowing God to be God. Her father, Robert J. Gore, shares his daughter's story.

God was supposed to see the note, not her mother and I. Kirby had carefully pasted the brief message on the flyleaf of her Bible. One of her sisters, snooping as teen-agers do, found the note. Her sister brought us the piece of bright-yellow stationery, saying that she felt it was important that we read the neatly printed thoughts.

As we stood there reading, Kirby's laughter came floating through the room from somewhere out in front of the house. When Kirby laughs, she laughs, she laughs loudly, and she means it.

The note read:

"Dear God—Please give me faith to be strong and to heal my body. Please make me a better person to be around. Dear Lord, please hold me. Love, Kirby"

There is no class for parents to take to prepare them for an accident like the one that put Kirby in the wheelchair. There is nothing that you can do to steel yourself for that telephone call.

"Come to the emergency room immediately—there's been a serious accident involving a member of your family. I'm sorry, we don't have any word on her condition at this point.

Kirby—16, tall, pretty and two weeks out of modeling school—was the passenger on a motorcycle. When the bike collided with a car, she was thrown into a low brick retaining wall. Her back was broken at the lower lumbar vertebra. She had no feeling or movement below the waist.

Although she can't remember anything now, Kirby never lost consciousness at the accident scene or during seven days . . . in intensive care.

She does have wide-eyed and wincing memories of 105 days in three hospitals.

Kirby is working hard to learn how to walk again. She may be able to walk for brief periods with the aid of braces, the doctors said. She has taught herself to stand, wobbling, and to crawl.

As she lifts herself from the floor to her wheelchair, her smile is bright enough so that her desiccated legs almost go unnoticed. Almost. . . .

(Gore, July 7, 1981).

The headline of the article affirmed, "The Lord *Is* Holding Kirby, After All."

Kirby teaches us about allowing God to be God. We can live in the lion's den if, with the psalmist we can say, "I keep the Lord always before me; because he is at my right hand, I shall not be moved."

Now back to my dogmatic statement. When we allow stress to control our lives, we are choosing another god, and we "multiply our sorrows." The Bible is full of promises of the healing, renewing, energizing power of God available to us. This is precisely the ministry of the Holy Spirit in our lives. And the Holy Spirit is the indwelling Christ. In John's gospel,

Jesus talks about his own death, telling the disciples that it is to their advantage "that I go away, for if I do not go away, the Counselor will not come to you" (John 16:7).

In the flesh, Jesus could not be with all of us always. Now, as the risen and ascended Lord, in the spirit as the Holy Spirit, he can be present. Not to claim that presence for forgiving, healing, renewing, energizing is to deny the most loving and extravagant offer Christ makes. To deny that presence is to practice a kind of practical atheism, to choose another god (the god of our own self, our own resources and strength) and thus to *multiply our sorrows*.

Reflecting and Recording

Recover in your mind two or three of the most difficult situations you have faced during the past year. Make a few notes to help you get them clearly in your mind.

Ask yourself the following question now, in relation to each of those situations. Did I claim the presence of Christ, his guidance and strength, in the situation, or did I simply muddle through on my own? Did I seek the counsel and guidance of Christian friends?

＊　＊　＊

If you claimed the presence of Christ, can you claim anything close to the psalmist's affirmation? "Therefore my heart is glad, and my soul rejoices; my body also dwells secure" (Psalm 16:9).

＊　＊　＊

If you didn't claim the presence of Christ, do you see the truth of the psalmist applied to your situation? "Those who choose another god multiply their sorrows" (v. 4).

＊　＊　＊

During the Day

Did you practice the instructions for yesterday? Read them again now as your suggestion for this day.

Day Seven: *Receive to Live—Receive to Give*

Jesus, knowing that the Father had given all things into his hands, and that he had come from God and was going to God, rose from supper, laid aside his garments, and girded himself with a towel. Then he poured water into a basin, and began to wash the disciples' feet, and to wipe them with the towel with which he was girded. He came to Simon Peter; and Peter said to him, "Lord, do you wash my feet?" Jesus answered him, "What I am doing you do not know now, but afterward you will understand." Peter said to him, "You shall never wash my feet." Jesus answered him, "If I do not wash you, you have no part in me." Simon Peter said to him, "Lord, not my feet only but also my hands and my head!"

—John 13:3–9

Try to picture yourself, with the disciples, in the room with Jesus. Are you shocked? We are the ones who should be on our knees washing feet, not Jesus.

About three months ago, my wife Jerry did a painting of Jesus washing Peter's feet. She tried to capture that decisive moment when Peter has drawn back from Jesus' act of love, and Jesus is speaking that awesomely challenging word, "If I do not wash you, you have no part in me." I have seen that painting almost daily since, and the truth Jerry sensitively sought to capture is growing on me. *I am united with Jesus only as I allow him to minister to me.* That's what Jerry was trying to communicate— that decisive moment, that profound truth: "If I do not wash you, you have no part in me."

Has it yet registered in your mind that before Jesus commanded the disciples to "wash one another's feet"—to serve others—he lovingly served each of them? Sure, he was modeling the style, defining the role of the Christian. But he was doing more. He was providing that nurturing, healing touch which would free and empower them to lovingly touch others and heal.

Are you trying to "wash the feet" of others when you are worn out, tired of stooping, and need help yourself—need a loving touch? Do you strain to reach out to others because you are inwardly in pain and depleted of energy? Do you continue doggedly to function though you know stress is about to claim the last resources you have?

Apart from human devastation, stress has become one of our nation's most expensive liabilities. Costs have been established at 75 billion dollars a year, about 750 dollars for every worker. Stress-related sickness is the major contributing factor, causing absenteeism and failure of workers to perform efficiently.

To be Christian is not only to receive Christ's message about the abundant life, but to claim his power to live it. *The power in him*—Christ living his life in us.

We began today by looking at Jesus in the Upper Room with his disciples, prior to his death, kneeling before each of them and washing their feet.

In chapter 21 of John's gospel there is a story with a twin message. It was after Jesus' death and resurrection. Before he challenged Peter to feed the hungry sheep of the world, he filled their nets with fish. Then, on the beach in the early morning, he cooked and served their breakfast.

Just as he knew they could not wash the feet of others, with all that implies, until they themselves had been ministered to, so they could not be sent as nurturing shepherds to the hungering, hurting world until they had been comforted, fed, given strength and the assurance of his presence, the Bread of Life always with them.

This is hard for us. It is hard to learn to receive. We like to be on the giving end. We like to be in control. It is not easy to admit that we are vulnerable, that we have needs, limits, and wounds. It is hard to admit it to others, and it is hard to admit it to God. Perhaps it is hardest of all to admit it to ourselves (Wuellner, p. 20).

The surest way to cope with stress is to claim and cultivate awareness of the indwelling Christ, allow him to be vividly alive in us, and to live out of his strength.

On Day Five, I introduced the soaking prayer. A similar form might be called the "prayer of the heart." For some, it will be an effective form of prayer for allowing Christ to minister to them.

It is a deeply incarnational form of prayer based on Jesus' parable of the yeast expanding within the bread (Matt. 13:33). Just as the soaking power envisages the light surrounding us and flowing through us, so this prayer envisages the healing power expanding from within. The heart is the symbol of the central energy flow of our bodies, just as it is the symbol, through the ages, of the deep center of God's love. In this prayer we are joining our physical and emotional need for renewal with the deep incarnational union between our hearts and God's heart (Wuellner, p. 21).

Reflecting and Recording

Practice now this form of prayer.

Place both hands, palms down, over your heart. (Your heart is central in your chest, under the breastbone.) Keep your hands on your heart in a relaxed position for a minute or two, and then say aloud or inwardly in silence, very slowly, with long pauses between each phrase: "The living heart of Jesus Christ is taking form within my heart . . . filling . . . calming . . . restoring . . . bringing new life." (Take a quiet pause, while you envision a warm light glowing in your heart.) "And this new life in my blood flows peacefully, with full healing power through my whole body." At this point you may feel like gently laying your hands on any part of your body that seems to need special help, and you may envision the new current of life through the transformed circulation flowing into that area.

When it seems right, open your hands, palms outward, and say: "And the power of this new life flows into my actions and relationships with others this day."

Then return your hands to your heart, giving thanks in the name of Christ, perhaps praying the beautiful words: "My heart and flesh sing for joy to the living God" (Psalm 84:2).

It is important that this prayer is not hurried. Move through it as slowly as feels natural. As you grow with it, you will probably wish to let it form its own timing (Wuellner, pp. 22–23).

You may find it meaningful to practice the *soaking prayer* at night and this *prayer of the heart* in the morning, as you begin the day. Practice both forms of prayer, adapt them as you find meaning, but by whatever means is effective for you, cultivate the presence of the indwelling Christ.

During the Day

Continue the practice of brief soaking prayer as suggested the two previous days.

Group Meeting for Week Three

Introduction

Two essential ingredients of a Christian fellowship are *feedback* and *follow-up*. Feedback is necessary to keep the group dynamic working positively for all participants. Follow-up is essential to express Christian concern and ministry.

The leader is primarily responsible for feedback in the group. All persons should be encouraged to share their feelings about how the group is functioning. Listening is crucial. To listen to another, as much as any other action, is a means of affirming that person. When we listen to another, we are saying, "You are important; I value you." It is also crucial to check out meaning in order that those who are sharing this pilgrimage may know that we really hear. We often mis-hear. "Are you saying _____?" is a good check question. It takes only a couple of persons in a group, who listen and give feedback in this fashion, to set the mood for the group.

Follow-up is the function of everyone. If we listen to what others are saying, we will discover needs and concerns beneath the surface, situations that deserve special prayer and attention. Make notes of these as the group shares. Follow up during the week with a telephone call, a written note of caring and encouragement, a visit. What distinguishes a Christian fellowship is *caring in action*. "My, how those Christians love one another!"

So follow up each week with others in the group.

Sharing Together

By this time, a significant amount of "knowing" exists in the group. Persons are feeling safe in the group, perhaps more willing to share. Still, there is no place for pressure. The leader, however, should be especially sensitive to those slow to share. Seek gently to coax them out. Every person is a gift to the group. The gift is fully revealed by sharing.

1. Begin the meeting by asking the group to respond to the image of "the lion's den." Is this a good metaphor for stress? What are some other descriptive images?

2. Take a good bit of time—as much as necessary—to allow as many people who will to talk about the stress they are feeling now or the most stressful experience they have had in the past three months. Hearing of others' experiences will help us identify our own.

3. Now focus on the experiences of stress that have been shared. Ask persons to be specific in identifying the different ways persons coped with stress. Have one person make a list of these ways of coping. When the sharing is complete, read the list, and see if there is anything to add.

4. On Day Two, we focused on the causes of stress. Reflect on the experiences of stress shared by the group, identifying any of the stress conditions listed on day two.

5. Pressure to perform, having our wants denied, and denying our feelings are major causes for stress. Ask if any person's recent stressful experience came from any of these.

6. Ask those who are willing to talk about things with which they are dealing which they feel are *beyond their control*. Some persons have difficulty sharing in this fashion. Don't force each other, but emphasize how important *acknowledging and naming* our stress points is to dealing with the pressure.

7. Look at the During the Day suggestion on Day Five. Did anyone experience the soaking prayer? What was it like? How did it work?

8. Look at the During the Day suggestion on Day Seven. Did anyone experience the prayer of the heart? What was it like? How did it work?

Praying Together

1. The leader should take up the polaroid pictures of the group, shuffle them, and let each person draw a new one.

2. Invite each member of the group to spend two minutes in quiet prayer for the person whose picture he or she has drawn, focusing on what the person has shared in this meeting.

3. Close the time with sentence prayers, praying specifically about the needs shared by persons when they talked about stress situations over which they felt they had no control.

Loneliness, Loss, Grief, and Death

Day One: *Fear of Abandonment*

Our focus this week is loneliness, loss, grief, and death. What a menu of problems and pain with which to cope! I lump them together because they are intimately connected. While we will deal with each specifically, we will do so mindful of their connectedness.

The underlying feeling that is ours in loneliness, loss, grief, and death is the fear of abandonment. This feeling is close to claustrophobia, the fear of being closed in, trapped in a small place. Many of us experience it in varying degrees. I get a hint of it when in a crowded elevator. Hardly ever am I in that situation without a thought striking terror in my heart: *What if this thing gets stuck!*

The fear of abandonment is akin to claustrophobia. Many of us not only live *with* this fear, we live *in* it a substantial part of our lives. Each one of us battles with the thought of being left where we are, who we are, with no way out.

The poet, Kenneth Patchen, expressed it this way in "Blood of the Son":

> Isn't all our dread a dread of being
> Just here? of being only this?
> Of having no other thing to become?
> Of having nowhere to go really
> But where we are?

Many of us express this fear in terms of being trapped:

- Trapped in a job that has become drudgery.
- Trapped in a marriage where love has died and neither partner is willing to take the radical steps and expend the energy demanded to breathe life into the lifeless relationship.
- Trapped at home with an ill and aged parent who demands constant care.
- Trapped at a point in midlife when you feel suspended, lose your grip on reality, and begin to respond irrationally to marriage and family and job. We call it midlife crisis.
- Trapped in the economic strictures of a business that has failed or investments that have plummeted to near nothing.
- Trapped in a dependent relationship where each person in the relationship feeds the weakness of the other.

The catalogue of entrapment situations and circumstances is nearly endless. It's the feeling expressed in the vernacular of Perry County, Mississippi, where I grew up: "I'm damned if I do, and damned if I don't."

Add to the feeling of being trapped a feeling of being abandoned and the problem is intensified, becoming even more devastating—bringing us to the brink of despair. What an emotional and spiritual onslaught—the fear of being trapped and the fear of being abandoned.

All too often, it is at times like these that we also feel abandoned by God. "Why dost thou stand afar off, O Lord? Why dost thou hide thyself in times of trouble?" (Psalm 10:1)

Have you ever felt that way? Have you ever wanted to say that to the Lord? I have. There have been times in my life when God seemed far off, beyond the reach of communication. I have awakened at three o'clock in the morning, morning after morning, and, anguished in spirit, prayed until daybreak; but my praying was more frustrating than fruitful. My passionate pleas seemed to bounce off the ceiling and ricochet around the walls.

It never shocks me when a person comes to my office and is hardly settled in his chair before he blurts out, "Preacher, I can't pray; there's no connection—I feel no presence. God has left me."

Anyone who reads the Bible shouldn't be shocked either—to hear that confession from another or feel it in his or her own soul. God's book, the Bible, serves us well as an opening to God, as a source to bring God nigh or to bring us nigh to God. The Bible reveals the anguish of many who felt that God was far off, absent, silent, beyond their reach.

The unknown writer of Psalm 10 expressed that feeling in words that resonate with the pain of a heart groping for God but unable to make contact. Hear the anguished questions that boil up from the depths of his despairing soul.

Why dost thou stand afar off, O Lord?
Why dost thou hide thyself in times of trouble?

To the tearful eye of (this) sufferer, the Lord seemed to *stand* still, as if he calmly looked on, and did not sympathize with his afflicted one. Nay, more, the Lord appeared to be *afar off,* no longer ''a very present help in trouble,'' but an inaccessible mountain, into which no man would be able to climb. The presence of God is the joy of his people, but any suspicion of his absence is distracting beyond measure (Spurgeon, p. 123).

''Why dost thou hide thyself in times of trouble?'' Spurgeon rightly reminds us that ''it is not the trouble, but the hiding of our Father's face, which cuts us to the quick.''

Reflecting and Recording

Beginning with the words suggested here, write two paragraphs describing experiences you have had. Describe the experiences in enough detail to recapture them.

I felt trapped when

I felt abandoned when

Look at both those experiences and see if you can recall how you overcame them, how you were delivered.

❋ ❋ ❋

Make some notes about your "deliverance" here.

Spend a few minutes in prayer, centering on the feelings of being trapped and the fear of abandonment and thanking God for the freedom and deliverance you have known.

During the Day

So many people feel trapped and abandoned. Maybe you do. But are there places where you feel free? Do you feel free in your marriage? Happy in your work? Fulfilled in relationships? Do you find meaning in school or volunteer activities? Go through this day recognizing those places and relationships where you *don't* feel trapped—and be grateful.

Day Two: *Share Honestly with God How You Feel*

Yesterday you were asked to locate some occasions or experiences in the past when you felt trapped or abandoned. As we begin today, bring that into the present. Search your mind and heart and be honest. Do you feel trapped or abandoned now? Describe the situation and your feelings.

A portion of Psalm 10 is a good place to focus now because it offers direction for coping when we feel loss—when we feel trapped and/or abandoned.

> Why dost thou stand afar off, O Lord?
>   Why dost thou hide thyself in times of trouble?
> In arrogance the wicked hotly pursue the poor;
>   let them be caught in the schemes which they have devised.
> —Psalm 10:1–2

> The Lord is king for ever and ever;
>   the nations shall perish from his land.
> O Lord, thou wilt hear the desire of the meek;
>   thou wilt strengthen their heart, thou wilt incline thy ear
> to do justice to the fatherless and the oppressed,
>   so that man who is of the earth may strike terror no more.
> —Psalm 10:16–18

The direction the psalmist gives us begins with *sharing honestly with God how we feel*. The psalmist insists on this.

We are not to be silent sufferers. Even though God seems far off, even though a large question mark is superimposed over our prayer, still we tell God how we feel.

God's absence is almost never felt when things are going well. Seas are smooth, the sky is bright, and we just assume that God is on hand taking care of God's own. But let the tensions build and frustrations mount, let life put its knee in your middle and start to pin you to the mat, and all of a sudden God seems to be gone. When this happens, do what the psalmist did. Tell God how you feel.

David Allan Hubbard, in his commentary on Psalm 10, provides a helpful line of thought.

Telling God how you feel will help because it will remind you that God is near enough to hear your complaints. God's program is not like a poorly managed restaurant. You know the kind—the food is cold and tasteless and the service is poor. When you try to complain to the waiter about the wretched food you can't even get his attention. Your frustration grows and your discontent mounts with every bite because you don't even have the satisfaction of making your distress known to the management.

The God of the psalmist is not like that. Though God may not be doing all that the psalmist wants when he wants it, he is within reach of the psalmist's prayer. The psalmist knows this and raises his complaint to God.

And he doesn't spare the details. What he feels he says. Thoroughly and forcefully, he describes his problem in all its ramifications. In verse after verse the psalmist reminds God of what his enemies are doing. Then earnestly, passionately he calls on God to act: "Arise, O Lord; lift up thy hand; forget not the afflicted." (Verse 12)

Listen to this, by telling God what he feels, he both unburdens his own spirit and expresses his trust in God. The psalmists were not silent sufferers. They took their complaints directly to headquarters, especially when they thought that headquarters was partly responsible for their complaints (Hubbard, pp. 26–27).

In sharing honestly with God how we feel, we both unburden our own spirit and we express our trust in God.

I've seen it happen so completely in corporate sharing and prayer. When a few people are together because they need each other and are seeking to grow in their Christian walk, release and relief come when some person breaks through his reservations or her fear of trusting feelings to others. For instance, to be able to say to another, "I'm afraid," is a relief valve with saving potential. The fear may have many causes.

"I'm afraid I'm going to die."

"I'm afraid my wife will never get well."

"I'm afraid that I'll take that drink or smoke that joint or pop that pill that will send me careening back into the darkness and helplessness of drug dependency."

"I'm afraid it has gone on too long—my indifference, my callous unconcern, my putting money and job and success above my family—I'm afraid it's too late, that I've lost my wife's and children's love. I'm afraid."

Fear is only one feeling. To be able to express to others these feelings of fear, or any other deep or tumultuous feelings that are about to explode within us, unburdens our spirit. It is dangerous to our physical as well as our emotional and spiritual health to keep those feelings bottled up inside. Sooner or later, they will break out—maybe as ulcers, or stress that brings a heart attack, or anxiety that brings a nervous collapse, or as rage that does harm to someone we love, or as loss of faith that undermines the possibility of spiritual healing.

Interestingly, sharing honestly our feelings with others is often the dynamic that will enable us to share those feelings with God. And when we do that, we are back at the needed place for further release and relief. We are back at the point of trusting God. So that is the insistence of the psalmist: *Share honestly with God how you feel.*

Reflecting and Recording

At the beginning of today's work, you were asked to describe a present situation in which you feel trapped or abandoned. Look back at that and make it a matter of prayer as you share honestly with God how you feel.

✳ ✳ ✳

If you have no present feelings of entrapment or abandonment, spend time in prayer of thanksgiving; also pray for those whom you know feel trapped and abandoned.

✳ ✳ ✳

During the Day

One of the things we discussed today is the benefit of sharing our feelings with others. Do you have bottled up feelings that might be relieved if you shared with another? Then do so today.

Day Three: *An Owl of the Waste Places*

> Hear my prayer, O Lord;
>   let my cry come to thee!
> Do not hide thy face from me
>   in the day of my distress!
> Incline thy ear to me;
>   answer me speedily in the day when I call!
>
> For my days pass away like smoke,
>   and my bones burn like a furnace.
> My heart is smitten like grass, and withered;
>   I forget to eat my bread.
> Because of my loud groaning
>   my bones cleave to my flesh.
> I am like a vulture of the wilderness,
>   like an owl of the waste places;

I lie awake,
  I am like a lonely bird on the housetop,
All the day my enemies taunt me,
  those who deride me use my name for a curse.
For I eat ashes like bread,
  and mingle tears with my drink,
because of my indignation and anger;
  for thou hast taken me up and thrown me away.
My days are like an evening shadow;
  I wither away like grass.

—Psalm 102: 1–11

There is no more poignant picture of loss and loneliness, of being cut off: "I am . . . like an owl of the waste places." The psalmist boldly colors the picture. "I lie awake, I am like a lonely bird on the housetop." "I . . . mingle tears with my drink." He even feels that God "hast taken me up and thrown me away."

Loneliness is the feeling that no one knows we exist. In its extreme, loneliness is the feeling that no one cares, not even God.

Where we are has nothing to do with it. How many people are around doesn't matter. It is the feeling of being cut off, disconnected. Phyllis Hobe has expressed loneliness in a fresh way.

Loneliness is the child in us, afraid of the darkness of an uncertain world. It is the infant crying out for the parent, longing for the comfort of strong arms around its vulnerable body.

Don't be ashamed of this child in you. It is a wonderful part of yourself. It connects you to God. It brought Jesus to His knees in Gethsemane when He suddenly felt alone among His closest friends. And the child in Him cried out to the Father in Heaven and received protection of a Parent's presence (Hobe, p. 97).

Loneliness is painful. The big feeling we get is that we don't matter. We would like to share our lives with those we love, but something gets in the way. Intimate sharing is essential for meaningful living. Without intimate sharing, we are lonely. The more cut off from intimate sharing we are, the more acute our loneliness.

There are two barriers to sharing of which we need to stay aware. One barrier is *feelings of inferiority*. These feelings are, more often than not, self-inflicted. They make us fearful of sharing. (What do I have to offer another? How will the other respond? I'll be embarrassed. She will turn me off.) So we allow our fears to shield us from taking risks of sharing in relationships.

The other barrier is almost the opposite. *We are not willing to acknowledge that we can't make it on our own.* Yet this is essential for a close relationship—to acknowledge need and be willing to receive what another has to offer.

All the teaching we have received, both subtly and overtly, mitigates against this. We are to be self-sufficient, at least to appear so. To admit hurt or need is a sign of weakness. If we expose a wound, or appear vulnerable, we are perceived as weak.

Who is the one person of whom we might say, "He didn't need anybody"? Jesus. Yet the New Testament records several instances when he shared his need with his disciples. There is one scene alive with the pathos of his need. Near the end of his life, when he knew the Cross was coming, he said to Peter, James and John, "My soul is very sorrowful, even to death; remain here and watch" (Mark 14:34).

They disappointed Jesus, slept while he prayed, but still he needed them to be with him.

Reflecting and Recording

Spend a few minutes reflecting on your own experience of loneliness. Are you guilty of putting up one of the primary barriers to relationship? Do you feel inferior or refuse to share your need?

✳   ✳   ✳

Recall and record here your most acute and/or devastating occasion of loneliness. Write enough to get in touch with the depth of that experience.

Summarize that experience by completing this sentence.

When I was so acutely lonely I felt like _____

Was some other person involved in helping free you from your loneliness? Write a name or names here.

_____   _____   _____   _____

What did they do?

Each of us has something to give. If you will look and listen, you will discover another who is lonely. The child in another will cry out to you. Hear that cry and respond. It will help you in your loneliness because two persons sharing together is an effective medicine for loneliness.

During the Day

Do you, even now, know a person who is lonely? Decide now how you will reach out to that person today.

If you don't know such a person, be especially attentive today. The chances are good that you will find one.

Day Four: *The Worst Thing about Pain*

Eugene C. Kennedy identifies the worst thing about pain.

It doesn't kill us; we never die of pain, although we sometimes wish that we could, if only to put an end to it. And the worst pains are those which seem to have no remedies, the ones that tear the edges of our spirit because they come when we are healthy rather than when we are sick. We may try to tranquilize these pains away, but eventually the ache returns. They even go on vacation with us, waiting for an idle moment, or a familiar song to use as an entrance into our hearts. What is this pain that will not kill us, this ache that has learned how to follow us so closely through life?'' (Kennedy, p. 38).

We all know at least a bit about the pains of simply being human and alive.

- A young person we know commits suicide.
- Our closest friends are getting a divorce.
- We lost our father to cancer when he was only sixty-two.
- One of our children was born with Down's syndrome.
- Our marriage partner has been unfaithful, involved in a sexual affair with another.
- Our parents have turned their backs against us, accusing us of not caring for them when in fact we are struggling to make it on our own in our marriage with little children.
- We have awakened to the fact that our spouse is an alcoholic.

Develop the list further. Record here four or five causes for pain you feel or that you see in others you know.

These ''pains of being human'' make us angry, cause us to grieve, send us into depression because we isolate ourselves and seek to bear the pain alone. The sense of loss often disconnects us from those we love, and we feel lonely, cut off.

It is important that we guard against guilt. Sometimes we become morbidly guilty about happenings over which we had no control. *We need to distinguish between sin that must be forgiven and painful wounds that need to be healed*. Flora Wuellner helps us here.

One way I have learned to distinguish between a sin that is to be forgiven and a wound that is to be healed is the way I feel after inner confession. When I have been confronting a sin, an act or decision of hurtfulness made in freedom of choice, I feel a sharp but releasing pain, like the lancing of an abscess. When I am confronting and trying to confess a wound, an act rising out of fear, phobia, pain, or unhealed memory, I feel no sharp sense of relief, and a dull pain continues to throb. Then I know that the problem is not sin needing to be forgiven but a genuine inner wound needing the touch of the Divine Physician (Wuellner, p. 15).

When this realization comes, guilt and heaviness are removed. We cannot bear the pain and seek healing of our inner wounds with the burden of guilt diverting or obstructing the process.

Reflecting and Recording

Go back to experiences I listed at the beginning of our work today—the pains that come by our simply being human and alive—and your additions to that list. Put a check ($\sqrt{}$) by each one you have experienced personally. Do that now.

✳ ✳ ✳

Now look at yourself. Are you still feeling pain from some of those experiences? Do you have an inner wound from these or other experiences that is yet unhealed? Hardly ever do you escape the dull ache of that inner wound. Most of us are there together, in need of healing of our inner wounds.

Joseph F. Schmidt, in *Praying Our Experiences,* has written helpfully about this process.

All our experiences possess a revelatory power, yet we find ourselves unable to reflect on some of them. They are too disconcerting. They are too hurtful. We do not want to feel again the pain. . . . We do not want to reopen wounds which have scarred over.

When we label these painful experiences ''wounds,'' we must remember that this is *our* label. We say they are injuries to our sensitivities, to our expectations, to our hopes, to our sense of propriety and dignity and success; but as they manifest a part of the truth about ourselves, they are not wounds but facets of the precious totality of our lives. Our prayer will be hindered to the extent that we cannot gather up all of the reality of our lives into our offering to God.

Prayer is fundamentally an offering of ourselves to God. . . . The parts of ourselves left out of our offering weaken our gift. God wants all of us, and so we work toward an integration of all of our memories and hopes into our total gift. To achieve this integrity requires that in some way the memories which cause pain and resistance must be healed. . . .

In acknowledging our painful experience as part of our personal history, we begin to open ourselves to the possibility of being nourished by God through that experience. To the extent that we deny an experience, however hurtful, we deny God's loving care, which is mysteriously embedded in that experience (Schmidt, pp. 21–22).

So to pray for healing painful inner wounds:

One, acknowledge the inner pain or painful memory.

Two, accept the fact that these wounds are a part of who you are as a person.

Three, this acceptance may call for forgiveness—either the need to forgive ourselves or another. This requires faith in God's love to bring healing out of pain, good out of evil.

Four, gratitude is the final step in the prayer for the healing of inner wounds. Genuine gratitude comes only when we accept the painful experience, the inner wound as a death that can lead to a resurrection. This is the way we say a new Yes to life which overcomes the No we have been saying in some particular area of our life.

During the Day

Sometime today, set aside the time to enter into prayer for the healing of inner wounds you have located in this exercise.

Day Five: *Grief*

> For everything there is a season,
>   and a time for every matter under heaven:
> a time to be born, and a time to die;
> a time to plant, and a time to pluck up what is planted;
> a time to kill, and a time to heal;
> a time to break down, and a time to build up;
> a time to weep, and a time to laugh;
> a time to mourn, and a time to dance.
> —Ecclesiastes 3:1–4

Grief is a universal experience. The time for grief comes to everyone. It comes from our loss. Common causes are the loss of a loved one—husband, wife, parent, or child.

But it may come from losses other than death. We may lose a loved one to drugs or alcohol, to a life completely foreign to ours which takes that loved one on a path that may never intersect ours. It is not uncommon at all for parents to lose their children in this fashion. They go a way the parents don't understand; parents can't walk that way, can't understand it though they desperately try. A wall is erected, estrangement takes place, and sometimes the loss is almost as painful as physical death.

More and more people today are experiencing loss through the incarceration of loved ones. Drugs is a primary cause. Just recently, we had a call at our church from a Christian family in Ohio. Their twenty-one-year-old son was in jail in Memphis and had requested a Bible; he was in jail for selling drugs. A painful loss for those parents nearly a thousand miles away.

Grief is a universal experience. How do we cope as Christians?

Common ways of coping are un-Christian and don't work. One of those is giving in to defeat—utter dejection, giving up. Sometimes we do this out of guilt. If death has occurred and we have wronged the person now dead without having righted that wrong or sought forgiveness, we may be overcome with remorse.

Another unwholesome way to handle grief is to let grief turn to anger and stay there. I say that very carefully. Anger at personal loss is natural. To express that anger is healthy. At heart, that anger is probably against God, though not explicitly identified as such. Let the anger come, and let it be expressed, but don't let grief stay as anger, and don't throw God away in anger. This will only add further loss to one that is already painfully bitter and hard to take.

Ann Kaiser Stearns reminds us that

anger is a struggle with holding on and letting go and it is a struggle with evil. We feel angry at the unfairness of life that we should have to suffer the loss we are facing. We feel angry at those who do not understand our pain and who appear to be so secure, safe and distant from knowing personally what our circumstance of suffering is all about. We feel angry at whoever or whatever is the cause of our loss, angry at one who dies for abandoning us. Not uncommonly, we feel angry at life in general. We search around for someone to blame (Stearns, p. 67).

Getting back to the previous point about anger against God, whether we recognize it or not, it is God to whom we direct questions reflecting our anger. "Why must I suffer? Where is the fairness in this? What meaning can there be? How can I survive?" We have been subtly taught that everything that happens is God's will. So, we hold God responsible— or at least we achingly wonder why God didn't prevent the suffering.

We don't need to be ashamed of our anger and bitter feelings. Expressing those feelings can help us move through our anger.

Now the positive. Express your grief. Cry. Share your tears with others. Don't try to hide or allow yourself to be smothered by the well-intentioned but misled folks who will try to keep you from expressing your pain in tears and/or confession of hurt. If you feel like screaming, not just crying, find a place and do so.

Don't let the pain of loss fester in resentment because you repress it. Any loss, especially the loss of a loved one, leaves a wound.

> It's a natural consequence. Because we do not want the ones we love to die, it's only natural that we grieve when they do. And grief can affect your outward life as well as your inward feelings. Perhaps you find it hard to be interested in your work or taking care of your family and household. Perhaps you are no longer able to think straight when it comes to decision-making. Perhaps you actually feel physical manifestations of your inner pain. The onslaught of grief can do these things to you. Be aware that they can. Start preparing yourself intellectually to meet them.
>
> When you are physically injured, you see the future as a time for healing. Allow the same necessity for an emotional wound. Don't say to yourself that you can't go on living without the one you've lost. Tell yourself, "I must go on, and I can." Keep ever in mind that the rest of your life awaits you. You've got some living yet to do (Miller, pp. 4–5).

Know that your grief is an entree and a binding to other suffering people. There is a fellowship in suffering that is redemptive.

> Thornton Wilder wrote a three-minute play entitled *The Angel That Troubled the Water.* It is based on the legend of the pool of Bethesda, where one could be healed by entering the pool when an angel appeared and stirred the water.
>
> There are three characters: a doctor with a secret burden, praying that the angel will come; a confirmed invalid, who has waited long for healing and upbraids the doctor for seeking the pool of healing: "You are able to walk about . . . Go back to work and leave these miracles to us who need them." The third character is the angel. Before he enters the pool of healing he speaks to the doctor:
>
>> Draw back, physician, this moment is not for you. . . . *Without your wound where would your power be?* It is your very remorse that makes your low voice tremble into the hearts of men. The very angels themselves cannot persuade the wretched and blundering children on earth as can one human being broken on the wheels of living. In Love's service only the wounded soldier can serve.
>
> . . . Your grief and suffering can be redemptive. It can transform your life. It can give you the sensitivity to listen, to share, to understand, to enter into the suffering of others with healing love (Dunnam, *The Sanctuary for Lent 1983,* p. 47).

We will consider more about grief, loss, and death tomorrow. For now one other word. In your grief, hold on to the love of God. It may be that the only way you can do that is to remember God's love on other occasions. Let that serve you now until the feeling-awareness of that love is real again.

Reflecting and Recording

Yesterday, we talked about praying our experiences and the prayer for healing painful inner wounds. Rehearse that prayer dynamic and use it now as you bring into focus some wound that you feel because of the loss of a loved one, however that loss has come.

During the Day

Do you know someone who is suffering? Take initiative in expressing love to that person today. One way to do that may be to share your own suffering. "In Love's service only the wounded . . . can serve."

Day Six: *Forgive God*

Have you noted the title of our focus today? Forgive God!

Does that shock you? Maybe repulse you? It did me the first time I heard it. Forgiveness is a response to wrongdoing and sin. God is perfect, Jesus himself teaches that (Matt. 5:48).

Forgive God! It's a nagging idea and gets our mind's attention because most of us have "found God guilty" for disappointments, losses, tragedies in lives. We approached this notion yesterday. When a loved one dies, a child rebels, a marriage fails, some crippling disease strikes, a baby is born handicapped, we cry out: "Why would God do it?—or allow it?" "If God really loved me, why would God let this happen?"

Our instinct in such circumstances is to summon God before the court of our personal judgment. We condemn him, judge him guilty for what we think he has done, and even imagine that by doing so we are punishing him.

God is innocent, but in our minds he is guilty. A wall of separation appears, built by our perceptions. Poison spreads in our minds and hearts as we judge God and hold him accountable. Such a foolish court scene, of course, does not change God or punish him, but it brings a seductively corrupting presence upon us and ultimately causes our relationship with God to fall apart.

Now here is where I believe we should ''forgive'' God—not for what he has done (for he has done nothing wrong), but for what we *perceive* he has or has not done. In other words, we must erase from our minds the grudge, or judgment, or whatever we would call it against our heavenly Father.

This forgiveness is not for God's benefit, but for ours. It does not cleanse a perfect God, or absolve him of something wrong, for he can do no wrong. But by ''forgiving'' God we cleanse ourselves, for we cleanse the memory banks of our minds and hearts of something that should not be there (Beers, p. 17).

Reflecting and Recording

Be kind to one another, tenderhearted, forgiving one another, as God in Christ forgave you.

—Ephesians 4:32

It may take more than you can muster, because the concept is so foreign to your thinking. And it may not be something needful. But think about it—and do it if you feel led. Look at past experiences. Are there wounds and pain that you have blamed on God? In prayer, very deliberately, forgive God.

During the Day

This notion of forgiving God is strange for most people. Is there someone you know who has been blaming God to whom you need to introduce this idea? Do so today.

Day Seven: *Joy Comes in the Morning*

I will extol thee, O Lord, for thou hast drawn me up,
  and hast not let my foes rejoice over me.
O Lord my God, I cried to thee for help,
  and thou hast healed me.
O Lord, thou hast brought up my soul from Sheol,
  restored me to life from among those gone down to the Pit.

Sing praises to the Lord, O you his saints,
  and give thanks to his holy name.
For his anger is but for a moment,
  and his favor is for a lifetime.
Weeping may tarry for the night,
  but joy comes with the morning.

—Psalm 30:1–5

I think it is my favorite line in all the Psalms: "Weeping may tarry for the night, but joy comes in the morning." It is a promise we need to hold on to.

One never *completely* recovers from a significant experience of loss; always certain emotional vulnerabilities remain. Most of us wear a coat with some grief in some of the pockets for the rest of our lives. But every pocket isn't filled with sorrow and the coat is supposed to become a lot less heavy from less unresolved grief in the pockets the older it becomes (Stearns, p. 152).

After making that observation Ann Kaiser Stearns shares a personal confession.

Sometimes the grief in the pockets becomes a problem. Old grief doesn't just lie dormant and harmless all of the time. On each of the several occasions that I have fallen in love with another man since my husband and I separated, the old grief has stirred around. There is the fear of another loss. . . .

One's perspective is permanently altered by an experience of loss: it's so easy, thereafter, to imagine catastrophes. A man who has half a dozen traits moderately resembling traits that were dominant in my husband's personality does not compare with my husband. In my mind, however, I fear the two are comparable, so I take seven giant steps backward. It's one of the ways that scars remain. Usually I will re-evaluate the situation, and I have been known to take seven giant steps forward again; but it doesn't happen automatically. Real effort is sometimes required to move against the fear (Stearns, p. 152–53).

What we need most to know and to keep foremost in awareness is the experience of God's love. But how do we do that? I have found four helps in doing so.

One, I need to immerse myself in the witness of the scripture.

The overwhelming message of Scripture is that God really loves us. We find it, in Scripture, over and over again—that God loves us, and that God's love reaches out to us, not as we might be if we were better, but as we are and where we are. Isaiah uses an emotion-laden image to picture God's love: "Can a mother forget her own baby and not love the child she bore? Even if a mother should forget her child, I will never forget you" (Isa. 49:15, TEV). . . .

A second help in my holding on to the experience of God's love is my memory.

The psalmists illustrate this over and over again. They talk about being "pricked in heart," of being "envious and arrogant," "afflicted and in pain," cast down "O my soul," . . . "like an owl in the waste places," shut in so that they cannot escape, eyes dimmed through sorrow. In the midst of cries of desolation and moans of despair they emerge in joyous exultation. The transition from sadness to song is *memory*, captured in a word like, *"I will call to mind the deeds of the Lord."*

It has been true for me. I can recall occasions when there was no doubt about it—God loves me. My conversion experience; the malignancy of my mother, in the midst of whose suffering the love of God sustained her and her family; a long period of recuperation following an auto accident that left me with a broken leg, broken ribs, and a punctured and collapsed lung—are all dramatic experiences, alive in my memory, which testify to God's love. . . .

A third help in keeping alive the awareness of God's love is my relationship with other persons through whom God expresses his love. . . .

Other persons as channels of God's love are essential for our journey. Much of the love, in fact I would be bold to say that *most* of the love that comes to me from others, is God's love coming to me through them.

When a person loves me in spite of myself; when I am loved though undeserving; when I have hurt another deeply, or have been callous to another's feelings and needs; when I have been insensitive to the pain and reaching-out of another, yet am loved and accepted, I experience this as God's love for me. . . .

A fourth help in holding on to the experience of God's love [is] the witness of God.

This witness is through events we store in our memory and return to, as I just mentioned. But there are also *nonevents*, experiences that may be labeled "mystical," or almost so. I'm talking about those usually momentary and fleeting occasions when, in the depths of our being, we hear it and feel it—God's affirmation of love (Dunnam, *The Sanctuary for Lent 1981*, pp. 8–11, adapted).

If we can hold on to the experience of God's love, we can cope with loneliness, loss, grief, and death. It won't mean that we won't suffer and cry. We will. But the psalmists' confidence will be ours. "Weeping may tarry for the night, but joy comes in the morning."

Reflecting and Recording

One of the ways by which we hold on to the experience of God's love is our *memory*. Ponder your own history. Recall one vivid experience of God's love, an occasion when you knew without doubt that God loved you. Record that experience here.

Our relationship with persons through whom God expresses love is a way of keeping alive the awareness of God's love. Who are two or three persons who have loved you in that fashion? Name them.

_____   _____   _____

During the Day

Contact those persons today and thank them for reminding you of God's love.

Group Meeting for Week Four

Introduction

Paul advised the Philippians to "let your conversation be as it becometh the gospel" (Phil. 1:27, KJV). Most of us have yet to see the dynamic potential of the conversation which takes place in an intentional group such as this. The Elizabethan word for *life* as used in the King James version is *conversation*, thus Paul's word to the Philippians. Life is found in communion with God and also in conversation with others.

Speaking and listening with this sort of deep meaning which communicates life is not easy. This week our emphasis has been on loneliness, loss, grief, and death. Some persons have had deep experiences of these—not easy to talk about. Therefore, listening and responding to what we hear is very important. To really hear another person may contribute to the healing process. To listen, then, is an act of love. When we listen in a way that makes a difference, we surrender ourselves to the other person, saying, "I will hear what you have to say and will receive you as I receive your words." When we speak in a way that makes a difference, we speak for the sake of others, thus we are contributing to the wholeness process.

Sharing Together

1. Begin your sharing time with a five-to-ten-minute discussion on the fear of abandonment as the underlying feeling in loneliness, loss, grief, and death.

2. Allow as many in the group who will to share an experience of feeling abandoned or of being "trapped."

3. On Day Three you were asked to get in touch with and describe your most acute and/or devastating occasion of loneliness. Ask those who are willing to share those experiences.

4. Perhaps others who don't share their lonely experiences will be willing to share the summary of their experience by reading the sentence they wrote on Day Three: "When I was so acutely lonely I felt like _____."

5. Spend a few minutes talking about the two barriers to sharing: feelings of inferiority and an unwillingness to acknowledge that we can't make it on our own. Refer to the experiences of loneliness that have been shared. Were there barriers operating in our lives to prevent us from reaching out of our loneliness to others?

6. On Day Four we noted the need to distinguish between sin that must be forgiven and painful wounds that need to be healed. Talk for a few minutes about how we confuse the two, thus getting no help for our pain.

7. Did anyone practice the prayer for the healing of inner wounds suggested on Day Four? Would someone share the experience with the group?

8. Let the group share about how they respond to the notion of "forgiving God." Be sure to move the discussion to personal experience. Maybe some have had that experience and will share it.

9. Close your sharing session by inviting those who will to share a vivid experience of God's love which confirms the fact that "joy comes in the morning."

Praying Together

Corporate prayer is one of the great blessings of Christian community. To affirm that is one thing: to experience it is another. To *experience* it we have to *experiment* with the possibility. Will you become a bit bolder now and experiment with the possibilities of corporate prayer by sharing more openly and intimately?

1. Let each person in the group share one need relating to loneliness or loss or grief or death. It may be a current situation they are facing or the pain from a past experience. As this is done, other persons in the group may find it helpful to take notes so that you can pray now and in the coming days in a more intentional way.

2. There is a sense in which, through this sharing, you have already been corporately praying. There is power, however, in a community on a common journey verbalizing thoughts and feelings to God in the presence of fellow pilgrims. Experiment with this possibility now.

    A. Let the leader call each person's name, pausing briefly after each name for some person in the group to offer a brief verbal prayer focused on what that person has shared. It should be as simple as, "Lord, give Jane relief from the loss she still feels over the death of _____," or "Loving God, give John the sense of your healing power in his pain over _____."

    B. When all names have been called and all persons prayed for, sit in silence for two minutes; be open to the strength of love that is ours in community. *Enjoy* being linked with persons who are mutually concerned.

3. If it seems appropriate, close this prayer time with the leader, or someone designated by the leader beforehand, leading the group in the prayer process for healing painful inner wounds, steps one through four on p. 97. The person doing this should have people sit comfortably with eyes closed, then simply read the steps slowly, giving time of silence about each to allow persons to actually do what the are being called to do. Close by simply saying, ''Amen.''

Depression

Day One: *The Miry Bog*

> I waited patiently for the Lord;
>   he inclined to me and heard my cry.
> He drew me up from the desolate pit,
>   out of the miry bog,
> and set my feet upon a rock,
>   making my steps secure.
>   —Psalm 40:1–2

Here is a powerful image—miry bog; more powerful yet if you know the swamps of south Mississippi or Louisiana. They call them bogs in Scotland and Ireland; we call them swamps or marshes. We connect the word with "down" to describe difficult situations. The car was *bogged down* in the sand or the mud. John is *bogged down* in his grief over the loss of his wife.

The psalmist communicates powerfully by using parallel images and repetition. "He drew me up from a desolate pit." Do you get that? Is that strong enough? Then try this: "Out of the miry bog"—now that's strong.

Bog is defined in the dictionary as "wet and spongy ground." *Mire*, as a noun, is even stronger. It is defined as "an area of wet, yielding earth, swampy ground—deep mud or slush."

So to make it as strong as possible, the psalmist puts those two together: miry bog. And that's a good description of depression which is what we want to look at this week. When we are depressed we feel we are in a desolate pit—bogged down in sadness and grief, in despondency and feelings of helplessness.

Depression is the most common emotional problem in America today. It is the "common cold" that threatens emotional wholeness. The hospitals are full of persons who are severely depressed. But those who are hospitalized, along with those who are under the care of a doctor for this malady, represent only a tiny portion of our population who are weighed down by depression and are functioning far below their maximum level of effectiveness as persons.

In the fourth century B.C., Hippocrates coined the term ''melancholia.'' We often refer to it as ''the blues'' or ''a slump'' or ''feeling gloomy.'' More accurately, the experience is depression. And it isn't just a problem of a particular class of people. Depression attacks the rich and the poor. It has no respect for race or nationality. Young people suffer almost as much as adults. (Did you know that suicide is the second leading cause for the death of teenagers?)

For some, depression is a sporadic occurrence; for others, it is chronic. For some it is severe, demanding professional medical and psychiatric help; for others, it is mild but still strong enough to make life tough and oppressive.

Severe depression makes us unable to function. Even in its milder form, it colors our lives gray, and robs us of joy and meaning.

Nathan S. Kline, a doctor who has been a pioneer in the biomedical treatment of depression, has written an illuminating book entitled *From Sad to Glad*. He gives this helpful perspective on depression.

> Depression might be defined as the magnified and inappropriate expression of some otherwise quite common emotional responses. That, of course, is true of many another disorders. By way of analogy, one expects to find heart palpitation in a person who has just run up a steep hill. Something is decidedly amiss, however, if such palpitation occurs during a sedate walk. So, too, with depression. All of us experience moments of sadness, loneliness, pessimism, and uncertainty as a natural reaction to particular circumstances. In the depressed person those feelings become all-pervasive; they can be triggered by the least incident or occur without evident connection to any outside cause. At times there may be a sudden burst of tears that the person cannot explain—or more or less constant weepiness'' (Kline, pp. 6–7).

As already indicated, the level of pain brought by depression varies. According to Dr. Kline, some persons are only vaguely aware that they ''feel blue most of the time.'' Depression expresses itself not so much as overt pain as the inability to experience pleasure.

For others the pain is acute. ''They may feel like bursting into tears when someone so much as looks at them. Some, indeed, do weep openly at the least provocation. Some withdraw deeply into themselves, becoming dull and lethargic, hiding the pain behind a mask that seems to exhibit no emotion at all. Some become frightened and irritable'' (Kline, p. 7).

Hardly anyone is immune. Most of us know depression; the difference is in degree. Please note that I do not presume to offer help to the severely depressed. Dr. Kline, quoted above, is committed to the biochemical treatment of depression because he believes that most cases of depression stem from a biochemical disorder. Even so, he acknowledges the mystery that severe depression holds for psychologists and psychiatrists. Such professionals are constantly revising their understanding of causes and treatment.

If you are severely depressed, you should seek professional help, and I would certainly recommend Dr. Kline's book.

What I want to deal with here is the "garden variety" of depression common to most of us. According to the degree, such depression is disabling, inhibits our action, robs us of vitality, upsets our secure patterns and rituals of daily life, erodes our confidence, distorts our perceptions, and intensifies even the mildest hints of guilt to make guilt unbearable. The depression most of us know may not be severe to the point of requiring medical treatment, but it still ravages our lives, bogs us down, and prevents us from experiencing the abundant life Christ offers. To cope with depression as Christians is one of our biggest challenges.

Reflecting and Recording

"He drew me up from the desolate pit, out of the miry bog." Can you identify with this image? Describe some situation in which you felt extremely "bogged down." Write enough about this situation to recapture the feelings you had.

In his book, *From Sad to Glad,* Dr. Kline listed the following as symptoms of depression found in his patients:

1. Reduced enjoyment and pleasure
2. Boredom
3. Rejection of opportunities
4. Poor concentration
5. Difficulty making decisions
6. Memory (failure)
7. Neglect of personal appearance
8. Retarded thinking
9. Social withdrawal
10. Fatigue
11. Insomnia
12. Ruminations
13. Remorse
14. Guilt
15. Financial concern
16. Loss of appetite and weight
17. Reduced sexual activity
18. Decreased love and affection
19. General loss of interest
20. Over-responsiveness
21. Fearfulness
22. Gloominess about the future
23. Anxiety
24. Irritability
25. Suicidal thoughts
26. Unusual thoughts and urges
27. Physical changes
28. Concern about dying
29. Need for relief

We are not interested in a clinical diagnosis, and I certainly don't want to play psychiatrist. But look at the experience you described above, and see if you don't see some of these symptoms. It will help you to try to look "objectively" at what is such a subjective experience.

During the Day

The affirmation of the psalmist was that God "set my feet upon a rock, making my steps secure. He put a new song in my mouth, a song of praise to our God" (Psalm 40:2–3).

Later we will consider praise as a way of dealing with depression. Praising God provides power for our lives and alters our perspective. Look for ways to praise God throughout the day.

Day Two: *Locate Yourself Honestly before God*

My God, my God, why hast thou forsaken me?
Why art thou so far from helping me, from the words of my groaning?
O my God, I cry by day, but thou dost not answer;
and by night, but find no rest.

Yet thou art holy,
  enthroned on the praises of Israel,
In thee our fathers trusted;
  they trusted, and thou didst deliver them.
To thee they cried, and were saved;
  in thee they trusted, and were not disappointed.

But I am a worm, and no man;
  scorned by men, and despised by the people.
All who see me mock at me,
  they make mouths at me, they wag their heads;
He committed his cause to the Lord: let him deliver him,
  let him rescue him, for he delights in him!

Yet thou art he who took me from the womb;
  thou didst keep me safe upon my mother's breasts.
Upon thee was I cast from my birth,
  and since my mother bore me thou hast been my God.
Be not far from me,
  for trouble is near
  and there is none to help.

Many bulls encompass me,
  strong bulls of Bashan surround me;
they open wide their mouths at me;
  like a ravening and roaring lion.

I am poured out like water,
  and all my bones are out of joint;
my heart is like wax,
  it is melted within my breast;
my strength is dried up like a potsherd,
  and my tongue cleaves to my jaws;
  thou dost lay me in the dust of death.

Yea, dogs are round about me;
  a company of evildoers encircle me;
  they have pierced my hands and feet—
I cannot count all my bones—
  they stare and gloat over me;
they divide my garments among them,
  and for my raiment they cast lots.

But thou, O Lord, be not far off!
  O thou my help, hasten to my aid!
Deliver my soul from the sword,
  my life from the power of the dog!
Save me from the mouth of the lion,
  my afflicted soul from the horns of the wild oxen!

I will tell of thy name to my brethren;
  in the midst of the congregation I will praise thee!
                    —Psalms 22: 1–22

You can't read this psalm without realizing the writer is sorely depressed. The first thing he says provides an insight for us in dealing with our depression. He expresses himself honestly. *He locates himself in* the presence of God. "My God, my God, why hast thou forsaken me?"

I remember a marvelous conversation I had with Father John Powell, a Jesuit priest who teaches at Loyola University in Chicago, and who is one of the most effective Christian communicators in the world today. We were doing a film conversation on prayer. As we talked about prayer, John Powell underscored the necessity for honestly locating ourselves before God. I never will forget the way he said it. Oftentimes when he wakes up in the morning, he finds it tremendously difficult to face the day, so he says verbally to the Lord, "Lord, I don't feel like being a priest today; I don't feel like being the town pump available to all who would come and make demands of me, and go away, taking what they wish, and often not even saying 'thank you.' I don't feel like being a town pump."

That's the sort of thing I'm talking about. We need to honestly locate ourselves before the Lord. The psalmist was completely honest. He even went beyond asking why God had forsaken him. He cried out, "Oh, my God, I cry by day, but thou dost not answer; and by night, but find no rest."

One of the problems with Christians is that we think there is something terribly wrong with our Christian experience if we admit that we're not on top. Somehow (and I think the devil has played a trick on us) the prevailing notion is that a Christian must always be glowing, always be on top, never down, and certainly never in doubt about God's presence. I think this shows how powerful the devil is, causing masses of Christians to adopt a model that even Jesus didn't fit. Do you remember Gethsemane? Sweat drops of blood, no less. Do you remember the cross? "My God, my God, why has thou forsaken me?"—the same word as the psalmist. No matter what our feelings of depression and despair, we are in good company. We need, then, to locate ourselves honestly before God if we are going to begin dealing with depression.

Here is a powerful contemporary illustration. Theodore Parker Ferris was one of the great Christian ministers of this century. Outwardly, his was a calm, serene spirit. He had a way of articulating the faith, both in his speaking and in his writing, that gave his listeners and readers courage and hope. After his death, some of his staff members were cleaning out his files. They came across a handwritten prayer. When on an airplane flight, he had written it on the back of a napkin.

Lord Jesus, I would like to be able to do myself the
　　things I help others do.
I can give them the confidence I myself do not have.
I can quiet their anxieties, not my own.

What do I lack?
Or is it in the way I am made?

I want to be free to move from place to
place without fear and I want to face the
thing to be done without panic. You did it,
and You made it possible for others to do.
You didn't count on drugs. You trusted your
Father. You didn't turn away from life,
nor did you seek pain or death. You met each
day as it came, and I would like to do the
same, but by myself I cannot.

I like to think that You can be with me, and
be in me, and that with your help I can do
better. This is what I hope for, and what
I ask for.

Clarence Forsberg, who shared this prayer in a sermon, said of Ferris:

I have his portrait on my study wall. I read his sermons faithfully and
marveled at the calm confidence and assurance that he communicated
through the spoken and printed word. I wanted to be like him. I wanted to
have the kind of poise and faith he had. I suspect that if you had visited
Trinity Church in the city of Boston when Theodore Parker Ferris was in
the pulpit, you would have come away with the feeling that countless
others felt. Here was a man with such deep confidence and faith that he
was immune to the ups and downs we experience. But, by his own
confession, he could help others to a confidence that he himself did not
always have (Forsberg, September 5, 1982).

Reflecting and Recording

Go back and read Dr. Kline's list of symptoms of depression in
yesterday's session. As you read them, put a check by some that trigger
feelings you may have. Then write a prayer here, telling God exactly how
you feel.

During the Day

Reread yesterday's During the Day instruction about praise and continue it today.

Day Three: *"I Am a Worm, and No Man"*

Go back to yesterday's text, and read the first eleven verses of Psalm 22. What graphic words: "But I am a worm, and no man; scorned by men, and despised by the people."

We continue to look at this psalm because it speaks so clearly and honestly to the problem of depression. Again, you can't read this psalm without realizing the writer was sorely depressed. One of the things that had happened to him happens also to us—*our self-worth is undermined.*

Whether low self-worth brings depression or depression brings low self-worth is a "which came first, the chicken or the egg" question. It is unresolvable. The connection, though, is tight—depression and feelings of worthlessness. "I am a worm, and no man," said the psalmist.

Fears that undermine self-worth are present in most of us. Check it out. Are you afraid that

- other people don't think you are attractive,
- you haven't been as successful as your peers,
- you often come off as dumb,
- you are so old that you are of no use any more,
- you are young and naive and people don't listen to you,
- you are not sexually attractive,
- you are too sexually obsessed,
- your education doesn't compare to your friend's,
- you are culturally unsophisticated,
- you are not as good a Christian as others think you are, or as you think you should be,
- God doesn't approve of you?

A part of the depression syndrome is allowing these fears to pervade our thinking, becoming preoccupied with them.

Somehow, we must lay hold of the truth that our value, our self-worth, is not in what we have or how we perform, but in who we are in relation to God and others. Meaning comes from belonging. One of my favorite verses of scripture is Luke 12:32: "Fear not, little flock, for it is your Father's good pleasure to give you the kingdom." Doesn't that lift your heart? What heartening hope! Whether we have money or not, are smart or pretty, cultured or corny, young or old, high performers or plodders—it doesn't matter. The kingdom belongs to us who belong to Christ.

Yet, it is not enough to know we belong. We need to realize that we are called to care. I doubt if there is anything that gives more meaning to our lives and is a greater antidote for depression than caring for someone and making a difference in that person's life. I am certain there is no greater joy than the feeling you have when you have been used by God.

A friend of mine, Dr. Ken Kinghorn, told of a friend of his named John. John is an ordinary sort of man in terms of education and wealth. Yet he is such a committed man and so perceptive in things of the spirit that he was invited to serve on the board of one of the outstanding Christian colleges of our land. On one occasion, the finance committee of the board on which he had been put was meeting. As was usually the case, the conversation got around to investments. Everybody was talking about their investments. Finally, the conversation focused on John and the question was, what were John's investments! Did he have any good ones?

Without guile and with a "convicting" simplicity, John said, "Oh yes, we've made some great investments that have really paid off. We brought a young girl over to the States from Africa. She lived with us for awhile, and we sent her to college and paid for her education. She's back in Africa now making a tremendous contribution to the church, as well as to her country. That was one of our good investments.

"Then there was Tim. He became involved in drugs, in fact, became the victim of drugs. No one seemed to be able to do anything about him; in fact, no one seemed to even care about him. We took him into our home, knowing it was a great risk. We didn't have any notion that we would be able to do much for him. But we felt called to try, to love him, and to give him a chance if he wanted it. Well, Tim is off drugs now. He's living a very creative and fruitful life. He married a few months ago, married a lovely Christian girl. He has a job, and he's able to support his wife. We look forward to his having a happy family. Tim was one of our better investments."

I'm sure John has bouts with depression, but my hunch is they are less frequent than in most of us. I'm sure he struggles at times with fears about self-worth, but I bet he doesn't give those fears much room in his life. John knows he belongs and that he is called to care.

Reflecting and Recording

Go back to the list of fears that undermine self-worth at the beginning of this session. Put a check by those you feel. Add to the list here. What are fears that undermine your feelings of self-worth?

Look at the fears you checked and those you may have added. How many of them could be annulled if you really claimed the fact that you belong to Christ? That he wants to give you the kingdom?

* * *

Could any of those fears be overcome if you would act on the conviction that you are called to care?

* * *

During the Day

"Fear not, little flock, for it is your Father's good pleasure to give you the kingdom" (Luke 12:32).

Memorize this verse. During the day, over and over again, repeat it to yourself, substituting your name for "little flock." "Fear not, _____, for it is your Father's good pleasure to give you the kingdom."

Day Four: *Be Totally Honest about Your Feelings*

Dr. Roy Menninger, psychiatrist, warned an audience of executives against the substitution of achievement for feeling. By idolizing prestige and immersing themselves in environments that stress results, Menninger said, many wind up believing "it is what they do, not what they feel, that makes them real, and that if they couldn't do those things no one would look up to them.

"Some never become aware of the fallacy of such thinking," he said. "Others are saved—by a divorce or a heart attack at age 44—by being forced to ask themselves where their values really lie." Most of those listening acknowledged, in later conversations, that they had no one to talk to.

It wasn't that there was no one to listen, but there was a dam that made one-half of a person a stranger to the other.

The famous physician-counselor went on to say that this isn't just a manager's disease. "Many people," he added, "don't recognize the feelings of anger, depression, grief and are not in touch with themselves" (Angell, pp. 16–17).

We are not in touch with ourselves if we are not in touch with our feelings. But it is not enough to be in touch with our feelings; we must be totally honest about them. The psalmist models this for us.

> As a hart longs for flowing streams,
> so longs my soul for thee, O God.
> My soul thirsts for God, for the living God.
> When shall I come and behold the face of God?
> My tears have been my food
> day and night,
> while men say to me continually,
> "Where is your God?"
>
> These things I remember,
> as I pour out my soul:
> how I went with the throng,
> and led them in procession to the house of God,
> with glad shouts and songs of thanksgiving,
> a multitude keeping festival.
> Why are you cast down, O my soul,
> and why are you disquieted within me?
> Hope in God; for I shall again praise him,
> my help and my God.
>
> My soul is cast down within me,
> therefore I remember thee
> from the land of Jordan and of Hermon,
> from Mount Mizar.
> Deep calls to deep
> at the thunder of thy cataracts;
> all thy waves and thy billows
> have gone over me.
> By day the Lord commands his steadfast love;
> and at night his song is with me,
> a prayer to the God of my life.

> I say to God, my rock;
>   "Why hast thou forgotten me?
> Why go I mourning
>   because of the oppression of the enemy?"
> As with a deadly wound in my body, my adversaries taunt me,
>   while they say to me continually, "Where is thy God?"
>
> Why are you cast down, O my soul,
>   and why are you disquieted within me?
> Hope in God; for I shall again praise him,
>   my help and my God.
>
> —Psalm 42

I don't know who this writer was, but he was depressed. He was a displaced person, living in a lonely place. Homesickness is a form of depression.

He was in a setting where he couldn't do the things he enjoyed. He talked about *remembering* music and festivals and celebrating with a lot of people. Something precious and meaningful was missing from his life. That can bring depression to anyone—change, break in routine, a sudden loss of the rituals and relationships that have given us happiness and meaning.

He was religious, and he felt estranged from God: "My soul thirsts for God . . . I say to God, my rock: 'why hast thou forsaken me?' "

When we are separated from worship, from our religious practices, it is easy to feel estranged and to get depressed. Many Christians experience that when they move from one place to another, until they feel "at home" with a new Christian community.

The writer of this psalm was so lonesome for his friends that it seemed everyone was hostile to him, sneering at him, taunting him about his faith.

Many symptoms of depression are here in the psalmist: fear of being displaced, out-of-step with his surroundings—not being able to do and enjoy what he had known and liked, the feeling that others don't care, that they may even be hostile—the feeling of estrangement. You wonder, with all this going on, why he asked that piercing question. He should have known the answer. Yet, he repeated it twice. "Why are you cast down, O my soul, and why are you disquieted within me?" He was depressed!

What stands out about this psalmist, what teaches us about dealing with depression, is that *he knew his feelings and he was totally honest in sharing them.*

One of the most helpful things to do when we feel depressed is to honestly share those feelings. That's tough for many. Some of us are afraid to think about things that depress us, much less share them. I learned recently that the man who wrote the popular World War I song

"Pack Up Your Troubles in Your Old Kit Bag, and Smile, Smile, Smile" committed suicide. The worst thing to do with our troubles is to "pack them up"—to bottle our feelings inside.

Alan Paton, the author who lives in South Africa, experienced a deep sense of loss when his wife died. His best known novel is *Cry the Beloved Country*. After his wife's death, something seemed to dry up within him. He lost the creative impulse. Finally he was able to talk about it. The way he did it was in a little book, in the form of a series of letters addressed to his wife. He calls it, *For You, Departed*. In the last chapter he says, "Something within me is waking from long sleep, and I want to live and move again. Some zest is returning to me, some immense gratefulness for those who love me, some strong wish to love them also. Writing this book has taught me to accept the joys and vicissitudes of life and to fall in love again with its strangeness and beauty and terror" (Forsberg, September 5, 1982).

We can share our feelings through prayer, talking out our feelings with God.

We can do it by journaling, writing it down. It doesn't have to be a formal journal. Even if that isn't our routine practice, we can do it when we feel a need—simply put down in writing on a piece of paper our feelings of depression, and what we think is depressing us.

We can share our feelings with a friend, a person we can trust, who is willing to listen. We can talk out our feelings, verbalize our depression.

Reflecting and Recording

Locate an issue in your life that has the potential of bringing depression. Or maybe the depression is already there. Describe the situation and be totally honest in expressing your feelings in writing here.

During the Day

Continue the practice suggested yesterday. Over and over again, claim the promise, "Fear not, _____, for it is your Father's good pleasure to give you the kingdom."

Day Five: *Stay Close to Significant Others*

We do not want you to be ignorant, brethren, of the affliction we experienced in Asia; for we were so utterly, unbearably crushed that we despaired of life itself. Why, we felt that we had received the sentence of death; but that was to make us rely not on ourselves but on God who raises the dead; he delivered us from so deadly a peril, and he will deliver us; on him we have set our hope that he will deliver us again. You also must help us by prayer, so that many will give thanks on our behalf for the blessing granted us in answer to many prayers.

—2 Corinthians 1:8–11

Though the Psalms, in their entirety, are the most graphic witness of honest, personal expression in the Bible, the balance of scripture is not without it. Together, the psalms are basically a prayer book while the rest of the Bible is history, biography, teaching, prophecy, poetry, parable, literature, etc. The Psalms model personal honesty, the crying out of the soul before God.

Again, the whole of the Bible offers this honest personal witness. In the above passage, Paul shares his life with his friends in Corinth. The picture is almost as dramatic as a psalmist in prayer. "We were so utterly, unbearably crushed that we despaired of life itself." One translation has that, "we were under great pressure, far beyond our ability to endure" (NIV).

Have you ever felt "under great pressure, far beyond [your] ability to endure"? I certainly have. We often feel *de*pressed, *sup*pressed, *re*pressed, *op*pressed. It is not difficult to believe that some enemy is after us. The *pressure* we are under—whether economic, moral, physical, relational—the pressure we are under produces the state of depression because we have been oppressed, or we have repressed or suppressed other feelings that now come back to us as depression.

Yesterday we considered the need to be totally honest about our feelings. Paul models this with his Corinthian friends. "We were so utterly, unbearably crushed that we despaired of life itself. Why, we felt that we had received the sentence of death." An expansion of the need-to-be-totally-honest principle is this: stay close to your significant others.

In one of the most helpful articles I have read, Raymond J. Council addressed the role of the pastor with the severely depressed. He suggested that the "central and fundamental role of the paster is to provide a supportive, consistent, and accepting relationship." He elaborated on this in a way that informs all of us, in our depression as well as in our relationship to those who are depressed.

> The pastor's presence is empowering because it provides a reality. For the severely depressed reality becomes distorted. Judgment is biased by the person's negative feelings and worsened by their isolation and withdrawal. The depressed person flounders without someone to serve as a touchstone, as a point of reference. The pastor's "being there" gives a relationship in which the depressed person can check, test out, and correct their perceptions. The pastor offers by his/her relaxed, patient, and attentive listening an environment in which depressed persons can re-establish their own sense of relatedness.
>
> Given the temperament of the depressed person, advice-giving, pep talks and exaggerated optimism are ill-advised. Giving advice as to what should be done only serves to increase their sense of personal inadequacy. Such an approach mistakingly assumes that with a little effort and self-discipline the person can rise above the morass of depression. Likewise, counseling the person to "pull themselves together" adds to the evidence of their inability to meet the demands of ordinary life.
>
> Quick reassurances are also a natural trap. Judgments that things are not as bad as they seem or could be worse or that the person has too much to be thankful for to be depressed, though meant to encourage, are harsh and futile. They reflect the pastor's disapproval by denying the seriousness and intensity of the experience.
>
> Finally, the pastor must be careful not to debate and argue about the feelings of guilt and worthlessness. It is highly unlikely that the emotions will be dissolved away by logic or reason and the attempt to do so may only tend to isolate the person further (Council, p. 1).

The role of the pastor underscores the general principle for all of us. To cope with depression we must stay close to our significant others. To help others cope, we must stay close as significant others for them.

This isn't easy, because in depression we often feel isolated and abandoned. Also, depression numbs our will power. The psalmist said, "I am poured out like water" (22:14), an image of not being in control, *wanting to will,* but not being able to act.

This makes it even more crucial for us to have significant others who will take initiative in relation to us, even when we may not *have the will* to take initiative in relation to them.

Reflecting and Recording

List here four significant others, at least two of them being outside your immediate family.

1. _____

2. _____

3. _____

4. _____

Do you stay close to these persons? Are you totally honest with them about your feelings? Would they take initiative in relation to you if it appeared that you had withdrawn from them? Think about each of them in light of these questions.

✳   ✳   ✳

Go back now and make some notes below each name. When did you last have a long conversation? What did you talk about? What deep feelings did you share that you had not shared with another? How did they respond? What did they share with you? Do this now.

* * *

Is there action you need to take to cultivate your relationship with these significant others to guarantee that they will be significant others when you need them most?

* * *

During the Day

Take some relational action toward your significant others, even if it is just a word or act of gratitude.

Day Six: *Use Memory to Affirm Confidence and Faith*

We looked at Psalm 22 on Day Two and Day Three of this week. Go back and read that psalm beginning on page 112.

* * *

Hardly is the mournful expression of his plight out of his lips ("My God, my God, why hast thou forsaken me?") before the psalmist reaches back in his memory and grabs hold of a truth, an experience on which he can hang his confidence and hope.

> In thee our fathers trusted;
>   they trusted, and thou didst deliver them.
> To thee they cried, and were saved;
>   in thee they trusted, and were not disappointed.
> Psalm 22:4–5

Here is a useful tool to help us cope with depession: *Use memory to affirm confidence and faith.*

One of the helpful things about the psalmist is that he keeps the struggle going. One affirmation of confidence and faith doesn't do it. Look at the pattern. It is an ongoing pattern of honestly locating ourselves before God, but desperately hanging on to the confidence and faith we know can be ours.

Depression and despair: "But I am a worm, and no man" (v. 6).
Confidence and faith: "Yet thou art he who took me from the womb; thou didst keep me safe upon my mother's breasts" (v. 9).
Depression and despair: "I am poured out like water" (v. 14).

Isn't that descriptive? And as bad as that is, it gets worse. Listen to the psalmist: "And all my bones are out of joint; my heart is like wax, it is melted within my breast; my strength is dried up like a potsherd, and my tongue cleaves to my jaws; thou dost lay me in the dust of death" (vv. 14–15).

Wow! What depression! But the struggle goes on, and the rhythm prevails.

Confidence and faith: "But thou, O Lord, be not far off! O thou my help, hasten to my aid!" (v. 19)

This is a very helpful insight offered by the psalmist. Many times, in our depression, we feel powerless, unable to act. Our faith is not alive; in fact, doubt is dominant. We find it difficult to pray with confidence. Our religious feelings are often dull. It may be that the only thing we can do is reach back in our memory and recall an experience when God was with us, when we felt God's presence, and were delivered from "the miry bog." Can you recall the time when days were bright and life was joyous? *By the exercise of memory, we can affirm confidence and faith.*

Reflecting and Recording

In memory, go back over your life. Recall and record here some experience when you were going through great difficulty, the pressure was on, you were not able to make it on your own strength, *and God was there.* In your difficulty, you felt Christ's presence, you found his love and strength, and you overcame. Write enough here and on the next page about the experience to relive it in your memory.

You may recall that you were asked to do a similar thing on Day Seven of Week Four. Select another experience to reflect upon here.

Offer a prayer of thanksgiving for the capacity of memory and for God's love in your life in the past. Affirm that love in your life now.

* * *

During the Day

Look for signs of God's love as you move through this day. Take some action, as suggested yesterday, toward your significant others, even if only a word or act of gratitude.

Day Seven: *The Call of Witness and Praise*

Raymond Council (to whom I referred on Day Five of this week) has outlined Psalm 22 to illustrate the classical symptoms of severe depression. I mentioned on the first day of this week that we were not going to consider severe depression and that I was making no presumption of offering help to the severely depressed. Even so, since depression is so pervasive in our culture, I think it is important for us to learn about depression so that we will be sensitive to it either in ourselves or in those around us.

(You may want to skip this material now and come back to it later when you have more time. If so go to this symbol (+) on page 129 to continue the theme of today.)

Council presents the striking similarities between the feelings in Psalm 22 and the classical symptoms of severe depression.

My God, my God, why hast thou   ISOLATION, ABANDONMENT
forsaken me? Why art thou so
far from helping me, from the
words of my groaning?

O my God, I cry by day, but thou dost not answer; and by night, but find no rest.	PSYCHOMOTOR AGITATION SLEEP DISORDER
But I am a worm and no man; scorned by men and despised by the people. All who see me mock me . . . they wag their heads, "He committed his cause to the Lord; let him deliver him, let him rescue him, for he delights in him!"	GUILT, LOW SELF-ESTEEM
Many bulls encompass me, strong bulls of Bashan surround me; they open wide their mouths at me, like a ravening and roaring lion.	PSYCHOMOTOR AGITATION
I am poured out like water and all my bones are out of joint; my heart is like wax, it is melted within my breast;	SOMATIC COMPLAINTS
my strength is dried up like a potsherd,	PSYCHOMOTOR RETARDATION
and my tongue cleaves to my jaws;	DRY MOUTH
thou dost lay me in the dust of death.	SUICIDAL IDEATION
Yea, dogs are round about me; a company of evildoers encircle me; they have pierced my hands and feet—	PSYCHOMOTOR AGITATION
I can count all my bones—	APPETITE DISORDER
they stare and gloat over me; they divide my garments among them, and for my raiment they cast lots.	PSYCHOMOTOR AGITATION

Some of the terms designating symptoms need explanation. *Psychomotor Retardation Agitation*—There is a significant loss of interest in and pleasure from activities (including sexual) which previously provided enjoyment. Appearing sad and hopeless, the person withdraws from family and friends. . . . They will often exhibit a wooden expression, perhaps walking or sitting stooped. . . . The depressed person may pace the floor, wring his or her hands, or ask the same questions repeatedly. Psychomotor agitation is evidenced as well by attitudes of antagonism, suspicion, and hostility.

Suicidal Ideation—Working with the [severely] depressed person presents a special problem in that there is the constant and real danger of suicide. This risk may also increase as the person improves, as he or she regains energy and will. The pastor should take seriously every expression of suicidal thinking, regardless of how vague and masked. Every suicidal gesture must be met with an immediate, decisive, and firm response. Because of this risk the pastor should never attempt to intervene alone. Referral is essential (Council, p. 1).

(+) Now to the theme for today: *the call to witness and praise.*

Psalm 22 continues to be our model. Despite the depth of despair to which he has gone, the psalmist says, "I will tell of thy name to my brethren; in the midst of the congregation I will praise thee."

The call is to witness and praise. The temptation of depression is to withdraw, to retreat into ourselves, to separate ourselves from friends— often to hide in alcohol or other drugs. The psalmist is *calling us out,* calling us to witness and praise.

As we considered yesterday, our witness may be only of that which God has done in the past. Rehearsing that will keep confidence and faith alive.

Memories transcend limitations of time and space. They permit our emotions to flow freely when the persons involved may be geographically remote, or even dead. One of the greatest things about memories is that they enable us to project a future which we can anticipate and celebrate. Such anticipation and celebration become the heart of our praise and witness.

Roger Watson, a member of our church, has written a joyful gospel song based on a prayer he heard an old man pray: "Lord, I know what you're gonna do, for I see what you've already done." Such witness and praise is our ultimate weapon against depression.

Reflecting and Recording

Ben Johnson has written helpfully about celebration.

I am most miserable when I cannot conjure up a memory which holds sufficient personal meaning to motivate me to move out of myself and invest my attention and energies elsewhere. Often, I have cured my diseased spirit by engaging in celebration. Celebration gives me the *courage to be* in spite of discouraging circumstances.

A friend who had become a Christian in his early forties became an ardent lay witness. For several years, he exuded a contagious spirit of joy and excitement. Then he experienced a series of devastating events. He suffered a heart attack, which blocked him from going on Lay Witness

Missions. And even as he lay abed recuperating from the heart attack, he learned via television that his father-in-law, a public figure, had died. A bit later, his mother-in-law discovered that she had terminal cancer. Recently, my friend recalled a conversation which he and I had during that dark stretch of time.

"You told me that there are times in our lives when we come up against mountains that we can't climb over—instead, we have to tunnel through them. As I've faced my mountains, I've found it's just as you said. Sometimes I find myself in a tunnel where I can't see light at either the entrance or the exit. When I find myself in this predicament, I think of my friends—people who really care about me. Their seeming presence with me warms my heart and illuminates my path. Soon I regain hope that I can make it."

There are times in my life when the spirit of celebration has evaporated. In such a time, I take the hands of my friends and the Lord. We walk together and soon life seems brighter. Again, I have reason to celebrate (Johnson, p. 142).

If you are in a group using this workbook, think of the stories that have been shared of God's renewing work in individual lives. Praise God for that. If you are not in a group, recall your own experiences and that of friends to make your praise of God a celebration.

During the Day

Find the opportunity to thank someone who has been a part of making your life brighter, who may have lifted you out of the miry bog, or kept you from sinking into it.

Group Meeting for Week Five

Introduction

You are drawing to the close of this workbook venture. This and your next meeting will be the last planned group meetings. Your group may want to discuss the future. Would the group like to stay together for a longer time? Are there resources (books, tapes, etc.) that the group would like to use corporately? If you are a part of the same church, is there some way you might share the experience you have had with others? Test the group to see if they would like to discuss future possibilities.

This week may be the most difficult to talk about—especially for those who need it most. There may have been more unfamiliar content this week than before. It will be tempting to share intellectually rather than relationally and experientially. Guard against that.

Sharing Together.

1. Begin your time together by the leader offering an opening prayer or calling on someone else (consulted ahead of time) to do so; then sing a chorus or a couple of verses of a hymn everyone knows.

2. Ask each person to share the most meaningful insight or experience gained from this week.

3. Ask the group to share their experiences of being "bogged down" which they described on Day One in Reflecting and Recording.

4. Talk about the tension you feel because of the expectation to always be *up* as a Christian. Is this a problem in your Christian community?

5. Invite two or three who are willing to share the prayers they wrote on Day Two. When the prayers have been shared, ask the group to respond by sharing their points of identity with the prayers, the feelings the prayers evoked.

6. Read the list of fears on page 116 that undermine self-worth and stimulate the pressure syndrome. As each is called, tally the number of people who checked it as something they have felt. Discuss the ones that were checked the most. Why are these our most common fears?

7. Check to see if anyone in the group would like to share the issue he/she identified in Reflecting and Recording on Day Four that threatens or is already causing depression.

Praying Together

Spontaneous conversational prayer—persons offering brief sentences— is a powerful dynamic in our group life. One person may offer a sentence or two now, then again after two or three others have prayed. One person's prayer may suggest another. Don't try to say everything in your one prayer. Pray pointedly, knowing you can pray again during this time of prayer. This way you can be spontaneous and not *strain* to make sure you have "covered all the bases."

Reflect on the sharing tonight, especially the sharing of "threatening" depression.

Before you begin actually praying, ask the group for specific prayer requests, especially for those outside your group who are experiencing depression. When the conversational prayer seems to have ended, close by inviting all to pray together the Lord's Prayer.

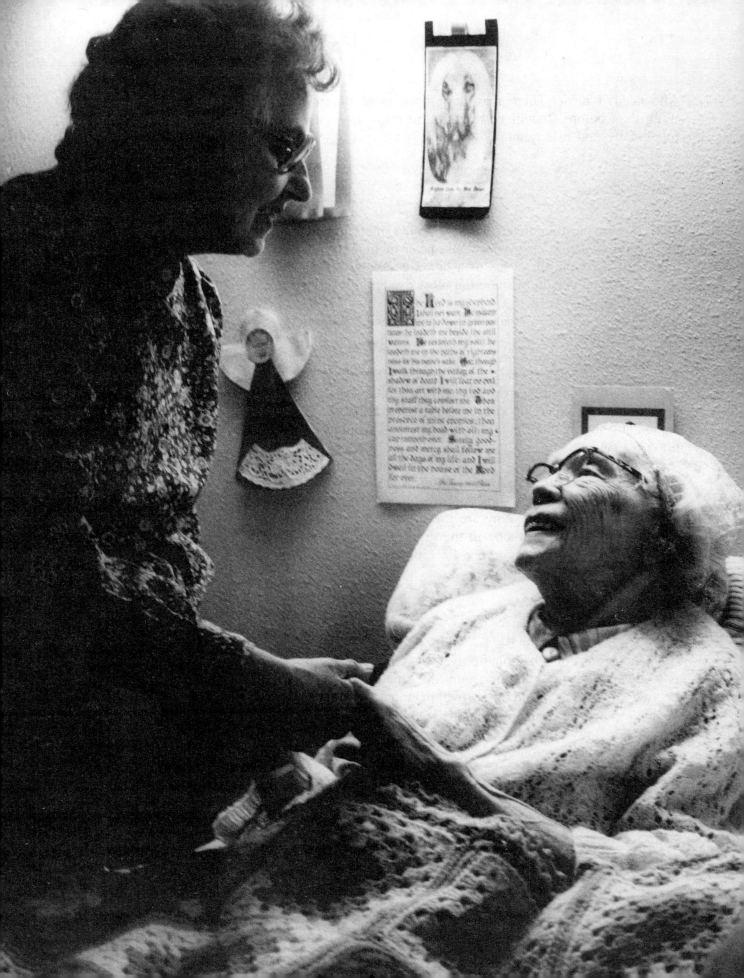

Compassion Fatigue and Everyday Demands

Day One: *Compassion—the Call of the Christian*

To be honest is a mark of maturity. Dishonesty has within it its own destructive seeds. Most of us know the huge amount of energy deceit requires. And many of us have discovered the awful devastation of living a lie.

During this week, especially the first days, we will deal with an issue about which we need to be honest: *compassion fatigue.* More directly put—we get worn out being Christian. For some, even to say that may sound un-Christian. The call to *being good* is so strong in our lives that we feel we are violating something very holy to even think about getting tired of being and doing good. I'm talking about coping with compassion fatigue—when being Christian has worn you down.

A mild little boy, not known for being ugly or mean, was being chastised and about to be punished for pulling a little girl's hair. His mother asked him, ''Son, why did you do it? That's not like you!'' ''Mommy,'' he responded, ''I just got tired of being good all the time.''

There is nothing out of the ordinary, and certainly nothing wrong, with recognizing the fact that we get tired of being good. The challenging newness of something diminishes, the sparkling freshness fades, things become routine. More than that, we get worn out. That's the meaning of fatigue. We don't have the energy to go on.

Let's look at that as it relates to the core of Christian living. Boil it all down, refine it to its most precious essence, and this is it: compassion is the call of every Christian.

You can open the New Testament to almost any page and find support for this thesis. This is what Jesus' life, ministry, death, and resurrection is about. Love. This is God's heart. ''For God so loved the world that he gave his only begotten Son, that whosoever believes in him should not

133

perish, but have everlasting life'' (John 3:16 KJV). There is a summary word of Jesus about it in the fifteenth chapter of John: ''This is my commandment, that you love one another as I have loved you. Greater love has no man than this, that a man lay down his life for his friends'' (vv. 12–13).

If you miss it as you read the stories of Jesus' life and ministry, then it is scathingly clear in that heart-piercing judgment picture of Jesus in Matthew 25. The basis on which we will be judged is made painfully clear. The basis? Compassion. Love and care for others. ''Come, O blessed of my Father, inherit the kingdom prepared for you from the foundation of the world; for I was hungry and you gave me food, I was thirsty and you gave me drink, I was a stranger, and you welcomed me, I was naked and you clothed me, I was sick and you visited me, I was in prison and you came to me'' (Matt. 25:34–36).

''But when did we do this?'' we might ask. And Jesus responds: ''As you did it to one of the least of these my brethren, you did it to me'' (v. 40).

If these small segments are not yet enough, let's focus on an entire passage of scripture, a simple, straightforward work of John in his first epistle. These words make up some of the most profound and exciting words in the whole Bible. In a very real sense, John has drawn together into one great set of sentences the whole theology of his letter and almost the whole theology of the New Testament.

Beloved, let us love one another; for love is of God, and he who loves is born of God and knows God. He who does not love, does not know God; for God is love. In this the love of God was made manifest among us, that God sent his only Son into the world, so that we might live through him. In this is love, not that we loved God but that he loved us and sent his Son to be the expiation for our sins. Beloved, if God so loved us, we also ought to love one another. No man has ever seen God; if we love one another, God abides in us and his love is perfected in us.

By this we know that we abide in him and he in us, because he has given us of his own Spirit. And we have seen and testify that the Father has sent his Son as the Savior of the world. Whoever confesses that Jesus is the Son of God, God abides in him, and he in God. So we know and believe the love God has for us. God is love, and he who abides in love abides in God, and God abides in him. In this is love perfected with us, that we may have confidence for the day of judgment, because as he is so are we in this world. There is no fear in love, but perfect love casts out fear. For fear has to do with punishment, and he who fears is not perfected in love. We love, because he first loved us. If any one says, ''I love God,'' and hates his brother, he is a liar; for he who does not love his brother whom he has seen, cannot love God whom he has not seen. And this commandment we have from him, that he who loves God should love his brother also.

—1 John 4:7–21

The powerful movement of this passage is like drumbeats. God is love. It is as simple as it is profound. This is who God is—love (v. 7).

God manifested that love by sending his Son into the world (v. 9). That's incarnation—God becoming one of us, personally identifying with us. "Love is the event in which God spoke for himself in human history by his son. . . . love, for John, is what God has done in our behalf. Love is the person Jesus Christ, alongside humanity, on the road as Saviour of the world" (Palmer, p. 67).

The rhythm of the scripture goes on. Not only incarnation but *redemption*, the cross, is here—the ultimate expression of love. "In this is love, not that we loved God but that he loved us and sent his Son to be the expiation for our sins" (v. 10).

We know what the love of God is only as we look at the cross of Jesus Christ. But there is more; the drumbeat becomes more strident. Looking at that cross, John concluded, and so must we, "If God so loved us, we also ought to love one another" (v. 11).

The drumbeat and the cadence go on, reaching an electrifying crescendo: "We love, because he first loved us. If anyone says, 'I love God,' and hates his brother, he is a liar" (vv. 19–20).

And then the summary, the bottom line: "And this commandment we have from him, that he who loves God should love his brother also" (v. 21).

So that is our call—the call to love. The scripture is clear. There is no other alternative. When you boil it all down, compassion is the style of the Christian—loving out of the love of God, loving with the love of God, continuing to love until we give up the last ounce of our being on behalf of the kingdom.

Now that wears us out. We get tired, we grow weary, and there's no end in sight. There is always someone standing by to be loved. There is always a loved one demanding more. There is always a stranger entering our life and causing us to sense that somehow in that stranger may be Jesus himself. There is always that call in the middle of the night, that request to go the second, even the third mile. There is that deep, unquestioned surging up within us, telling us we have to do it, we have to give that cup of cold water in Jesus' name. The call to love demands our energy. It drains us of power. And so, we grow weary. We suffer compassion fatigue.

Reflecting and Recording

Have you ever been tired of being and doing good? Have you ever sincerely admitted that to yourself? Have you ever confessed that to God? Have you ever shared it with someone else?

Spend some time reflecting on the call to compassion and the weariness you may sometimes feel in responding. Be honest. As Christians, we do well to consistently examine our style. If we are living the compassionate life to which Jesus calls, I can't imagine that we won't sometimes overextend ourselves.

✳ ✳ ✳

During the Day

Pay attention to this day in light of Jesus' call to love. Are you responding? Are you responding too much?

Day Two: *A Rabbit on the Swim Team*

Once upon a time, the animals decided they should do something meaningful to meet the problems of the new world. So they organized a school.

They adopted an activity curriculum of running, climbing, swimming, and flying. To make it easier to administer the curriculum, all the animals took all the subjects.

The duck was excellent in swimming, in fact, better than his instructor. But he made only passing grades in flying and was very poor in running. Since he was slow in running, he had to drop swimming and stay after school to practice running. This caused his web feet to be badly worn, so that he was only average in swimming. But average was quite acceptable, so nobody worried about that—except the duck.

The rabbit started at the top of his class in running, but developed a nervous twitch in his leg muscles because of so much make-up work in swimming.

The squirrel was excellent in climbing, but he encountered constant frustration in flying class because his teacher made him start from the ground up instead of from the treetop down. He developed charley horses from overexertion, and so only got a C in climbing and a D in running.

The eagle was a problem child and was severely disciplined for being a nonconformist. In climbing classes, he beat all the others to the top of the tree, but insisted on using his own way to get there. . . .

The obvious moral of the story is a simple one. Each creature has its

own set of capabilities in which it will naturally excel—unless it is expected or forced to fit a mold it doesn't fit. When that happens, frustration, discouragement, and even guilt bring overall mediocrity or complete defeat.

I heard Chuck Swindoll tell that parable, and it has stayed with me, not because of its humor but because it is enlightening and encouraging for Christians who experience compassion fatigue.

I hope I made the case clear yesterday: the call to love is Jesus' primary call. His style is compassionate. In a few verses, Mark gives us a picture of Jesus which shows his compassion but also gives us some guidance about compassion fatigue.

> The apostles returned to Jesus, and told him all that they had done and taught. And he said to them, "Come away by yourselves to a lonely place, and rest a while." For many were coming and going, and they had no leisure even to eat. And they went away in the boat to a lonely place by themselves. Now many saw them going, and knew them, and they ran there on foot from all the towns, and got there ahead of them. As he went ashore he saw a great throng, and he had compassion on them, because they were like sheep without a shepherd; and he began to teach them many things.
>
> —Mark 6:30–34

Jesus had compassion, but he also knew the need to rest. This should at least free our minds a bit so that we can think clearly about compassion fatigue and not feel guilty about being tired in the Lord's work.

So we press the question now. How do we deal with it? How do we cope? How do we continue when being Christian has worn us down? *We must recognize that there is a limit to what we can offer.* Chuck Swindoll's parable makes the point humorously. But it is tough—tough for sincere Christians to recognize that there is a limit to what we can offer.

God has given so much to us, and we're so grateful. Our love sensitizes us to needs around us. The more we love, the more aware we become of the need for love. The closer we walk with the Lord, the more our eyes are opened, and the more we see the loneliness and pain, the quiet desperation of people around us, reaching out—hoping that someone will see, hear and then stop and listen and touch. The closer we walk with the Lord, the more tender our hearts become, and we cry within when need goes unmet.

Then our consciences burn when we don't respond, when we fail, when we cannot do all that needs to be done.

So it's tough—so very tough for the sincere Christian to recognize that there is a limit to what we can offer.

Reflecting and Recording

On the lines below list the three people you know personally who, in your mind, live the compassionate style of Jesus most effectively and attractively—persons who genuinely reflect Jesus' call to love as he has loved. Do that now before you read on.

_____

_____

_____

Now go back and write two or three sentences describing these persons and what they do.

✳   ✳   ✳

Think about these persons in terms of their energy to keep going, how they cope. Have you seen them weary? Have they ever confessed being worn out? Do you suppose they recognize that there is a limit to what they can offer?

✳   ✳   ✳

Offer now a prayer of thanksgiving for these persons, and also pray that the Lord may teach you, through them, about being a person of compassion.

✳   ✳   ✳

During the Day

If possible, talk to one of the persons you named above. Tell them what you are doing, and why you are thinking about them. Then ask them what they do about compassion fatigue.

If you can't talk personally to one of these persons, write a letter. Select someone else (not necessarily a model) simply to talk with about the matter of compassion fatigue.

Day Three: *Leave to God and Others What You Cannot Do*

Dr. Roland Walker was a professor of Bible and religion at Ohio Wesleyan University. He inspired countless young men and women with his teaching. He confessed that he had to go through a lot of doubt and despair before he came to realize in its depth the steadfast love of the Eternal and how he had to function in relation to God. He told of rising one morning at one o'clock, going in to his study, taking his pen, and writing the following letter:

To the Governing General of the Universe
Dear Sir:
I hereby resign my self-appointed position as directing superintendent of my own life and of the world. I cannot level all the mountains of injustice, or fill in all the valleys of selfishness. There's too much of it in me. I hereby turn over to you for your disposition and use my life, my money, my time, and talents, to be at your disposal.
Your respectful and obedient servant,
Roland Walker

It is a significant turning point in our lives when we begin to realize that we can't do everything, and we are given the grace to relax in the fact that we can leave to God and to others what we can't do ourselves.

Yesterday we suggested that the first thing we need to learn in order to cope with compassion fatigue is to recognize that *there is a limit to what we can offer*. Today we consider a second suggestion. *Relax in the fact that there is a time to leave to God and to others what we cannot do*. Paul gave us a marvelous picture of this.

What then is Apollos? What is Paul? Servants through whom you believed, as the Lord assigned to each. I planted, Apollos watered, but God gave the growth. So neither he who plants nor he who waters is anything, but only God who gives the growth. He who plants and he who waters are equal, and each shall receive his wages according to his labor. For we are God's fellow workers; you are God's field, God's building.

—1 Corinthians 3:5–9

We need to learn that we are not solo workers in God's vineyard. There are other workers, and God guarantees the growth and the harvest. To learn this well will not only help us *overcome* compassion fatigue, it will be a *preventive* force, keeping us from getting to the point of fatigue. This is not a lesson we learn once and for all. We have to keep reminding ourselves of it and keep acting on it over and over again.

I confess that this is a big problem in my life. Hardly a week passes that I'm not so burdened by the cares and concerns of my congregation that two or three mornings a week, I will awaken at two or three o'clock and begin to think about those persons with whom I've been sharing or with whom I would like to share.

My mind focuses on the young mother who is waging a courageous battle against cancer, on her two little children and her husband who need her and love her and can't understand the awful blow that has struck.

I think about the couple who have just lost their beautiful college-age daughter in an auto accident. How can I speak to such mindless cruelty?

Thoughts of the fifty-year-old man who is wrestling with depression fill my mind. The rug of his business life has been pulled out from under him, and he has been sent sprawling to the floor. He is confused and hurt because supposed friends have betrayed him, worried because he has put most of his financial eggs in this one basket and that basket seems to have a hole in it.

How can I help the couple who have gone their selfish ways for so long that they've almost destroyed their marriage? Now when the shock of what they have done to each other, and the awareness of what they're losing, comes to them, they desperately seek help—help that is hard to give because selfish patterns of relating are so galvanized that they find it almost impossible to even see the problem, much less act to resolve it.

Sometimes I lie for an hour or two in sleepless anguish, wishing I were three or four people rather than one, wishing there were forty hours rather than twenty-four in the day, wishing that I had bushels rather than pints of spiritual guidance and support to pass around.

I confess I don't handle it well, but I know the answer. I keep reminding myself that I can relax a bit if I can believe that the time comes to leave to God and others what I cannot do myself.

The most jolting thing I say to myself, and it pulls me up short and causes me to think more clearly, is this: "Maxie, you cannot be God."

It's tempting to try, isn't it? Also, it's difficult to remember that ours are not the only hands and feet Christ has; there are others who share his life and ministry. I believe that Edward Hale had the answer in his poem, "Lend a Hand":

> I am only one,
> But still I am one.
> I cannot do everything,
> But still I can do something;
> And because I cannot do everything
> I will not refuse to do the something that I can do.

That's the only sensible way to live, doing the very best we can, loving as much as we can love, spending what energy we have, but trusting God and others to do the rest.

Reflecting and Recording

Think of your current most difficult involvements and/or tasks, that for which you feel a heavy burden of responsibility. In a word or two, designate those now to get them into focus.

Look at each of them. Do you need to apply either of the suggestions for coping with compassion fatigue?

Recognize that there is a limit to what we can offer.

Relax in the fact that we can leave to God and others what we can't do ourselves.

Spend some prayerful time reflecting on the demanding involvements of your life in the light of these principles.

✳ ✳ ✳

During the Day

Were you able to follow through on yesterday's suggestion to talk with or write one of your models for Christlike compassion? If not, do so today.

If you did, find another person, not necessarily a model, to talk with about compassion fatigue. Share these coping suggestions and get that person's responses.

Day Four: *Waiting on the Lord*

> Why do you say, O Jacob,
> and speak, O Israel,
> "My way is hid from the Lord,
> and my right is disregarded by my God"?
> Have you not known? Have you not heard?
> The Lord is the everlasting God,
> the Creator of the ends of the earth.
> He does not faint or grow weary,
> his understanding is unsearchable.
> He gives power to the faint,
> and to him who has no might he increases strength.
> Even youths shall faint and be weary,
> and young men shall fall exhausted;
> but they who wait for the Lord shall renew their strength,
> they shall mount up with wings like eagles,
> they shall run and not be weary,
> they shall walk and not faint.
> —Isaiah 40: 27–31

This word from Isaiah suggests a third help for coping with compassion fatigue: *renew your strength by waiting on the Lord.*

Christians need to realize that we cannot act out of our own strength alone. We must establish a pace in life, a rhythm of engagement and disengagement—being in the world but removing ourselves from the world—in order that we might be renewed.

When we go in our own strength, we soon run out. Here a crucial understanding of the Christian faith must be underscored. *There is a difference between following Christ and being in Christ.* To be in Christ was Paul's favorite definition of a Christian. "Therefore, if any one is in Christ, he is a new creation; the old has passed away, behold, the new has come" (2 Cor. 5:17). Jesus called us to abide in him. "I am the vine, you are the branches. He who abides in me, and I in him, he it is that bears much fruit, for apart from me you can do nothing" (John 15:5).

This has been the major failure of Christians from the second century on. We have emphasized following Jesus as the heart of Christianity, thus we tend to reduce Christianity to a religion of morals and ethics, denuding it of its power. Following Jesus is important. That is what we are called to do. But the point is this: we cannot follow Jesus for long unless we are in Christ, unless we are abiding in him. So, we renew our strength by waiting on the Lord, by spending time in his presence in prayer, with his word, with his people, cultivating the presence of Christ within us in order that we act in the world out of his indwelling Spirit which empowers us.

Some may remember twenty-five years ago an atomic submarine that disappeared in the depths of the ocean. It was named the USS *Thresher.* People never knew why it went down. They surmised that it had gone so deep that it simply went out of control. It was designed only to go to certain depths.

Some years after it disappeared, because of the perfection of technology, we were able to send another submarine down, a small one—thick glass, thick-plated, highly pressurized, and oxygen equipped to go much deeper than the *Thresher* had been able to go.

When they found the *Thresher,* they discovered it had exploded on itself. It had suffered an implosion, and this hunk of steel was like a crushed piece of paper. The pressure within it was obviously not able to withstand the pressure without.

There was an even more surprising thing in that deep-sea environment. Swimming about the crushed submarine were sea creatures. They had big eyes, their skin was very thin, and yet they were living in the same environment that had crushed the huge steel machine on itself. How could they survive in that pressure? Scientists told us that inside these sea creatures was an opposite and equal pressure to that which was without them.

This story is a modern parable for us. The indwelling Christ is to be cultivated to the point that inside us his power prevails and gives us the strength to go on when our own strength fails. We can survive the *doing* of our Christianity if the *being* of our Christian life is kept intact and up-to-date.

Reflecting and Recording

The three suggestions we have made for coping with compassion fatigue are:

1. Recognize that there is a limit to what we can offer.
2. Relax in the fact that we can leave to God and others what we can't do ourselves.
3. Renew our strength by waiting on the Lord.

Look back at the three people you named on Day Two as models for the compassion style of Jesus. Are these principles incorporated in their lives?

✳ ✳ ✳

Think of the models and the persons with whom you have talked about coping with compassion fatigue. Are there suggestions you can add to the three I have offered? List them here.

Spend some time in prayer now, simply resting in the Lord. Be quiet in Christ's presence, affirming that he lives within you.

During the Day

If you are a part of a sharing group, think about the members of that group. Are there particular ones whom you think may be suffering compassion fatigue or on the verge of it? Call them and offer a word of encouragement.

If you are not in a group, think of someone you know who needs a word of encouragement at this point.

Day Five: *Managing Time*

Owe no one anything, except to love one another; for he who loves his neighbor has fulfilled the law.

—Romans 13:8

This is Paul reiterating what Jesus made so clear, that the primary call of Christians is to love. The New English Bible translates a portion of the above verse, "Leave no claim outstanding, except that of mutual love."

That means we never get through paying the debt of love. That obligation is always outstanding, and that creates one of the pressure points of our daily living. *How do we manage time?* We feel the pressure to meet all obligations, to give time to our family and friends, to spend talent and energy in worthy causes.

A fine Christian man, David Lazell, . . . wrote, "By the time you read this, I will be in a mental hospital. As I pack my bags for my stay in the mental hospital, I wonder if it would have been necessary, if, instead of being a willing horse, I had been just part of a team. That is the question that faces every Christian worker sooner or later. We are not made to take too much pressure on our own. The Lord will have us rest, even if it takes a nervous breakdown to do it."

David found he could no longer cope under the pressure of those things that were expected of him. Fortunately, after a short stay in hospital, he was soon able once more to continue his normal life. With encouragement, counselling and a redistribution of his workload, he has been able to cope ever since (Moyes, p. 96).

Our situations may not be so dramatic or our cures so complete. Many of us still feel harassed by the pressures that come from demands on our time.

Books have been written about time management, and corporations spend thousands of dollars sending their executives to seminars to learn how to manage time. Time is a priceless commodity. It is the precious essence of life. Yet, in this workbook on coping we are giving it only slight focused attention. There is a sense in which everything in this workbook is about time management. The pressure of time is a part of all our problems, even the problem of loneliness when time hangs heavy, when we think we have "time on our hands" and wish we had more to do.

I want to focus on a dimension of the time management problem which relates to the theme we have been considering this week, compassion fatigue. Sure, we need to plan our use of time. We need to make lists of "things to do today." We need to set aside specific time for recreation and being with our mates in marriage. We must not ignore giving quality time to our children, and this requires intentionality. Time management is basically a matter of planning.

But—and what a big reservation this is—planning doesn't relieve us of the pressure. The claim is still there. "Leave no claim outstanding, except that of mutual love."

If we are sincere in living the style of Jesus with compassion as the driving force of our lives, the debt of love is always outstanding.

Here is a confrontational fact. *Paying the debt of love can turn us into neurotic, driven people.* How do we prevent this from happening, or change it if it already has? James W. Angell has suggested an overall framework.

> Even if we should find it possible to settle most of our obligations, we can't pay them all. Nor should we want to. It is no achievement to be entirely free of debt, or trumpet such nonsense as "I don't owe anybody anything." What child could repay his parents? Life is no quid pro quo. It is needing one another. It isn't being "paid up"; it's living with a permanent "accounts payable" (Angell, p. 70).

It's not easy, but we must find that grace—the grace of living with a permanent "accounts payable."

To help us with that I add this suggestion. We must become "selfish" and spend time with people we like and who energize us. Author Jess Lair, in his book, *I Ain't Much, Baby, But I'm All I've Got,* is one who ignited this truth for me. He bemoans the fact that many of us, out of guilt, spend a lot of our time with difficult people who are very hard to like, who drain us of energy but give nothing back to restore us. Neither Lair nor I would minimize the need for caring for all sorts of people. Jesus wasn't selective about the pleas of need which came to him, nor can we be. That makes it all the more important that we "selfishly" plan to be with people we like, people who energize us, who mean a lot to us and whose company is a renewing experience.

On the surface it seems selfish, but it may be the biggest thing we do to guarantee survival.

Reflecting and Recording

List below all the people you can think of, apart from the persons involved with you during your workday, with whom you have spent thirty minutes or more during the past two weeks. Put a (√) by the persons who drained energy from you and an (×) by those who energized you.

NAME	DRAINED (√)	ENERGIZED (×)

What do you think of the balance? Are you not giving yourself enough to the claim of mutual love? Are you driven too much to pay the debt of love and not being renewed by spending time with those who renew and energize you?

During the Day

Do one of two things today—maybe both. Make an appointment to spend some time with a favorite person (apart from your family) and/or call one of your favorite persons, tell them what you have been considering today, and thank them for being one of the persons who provides renewal and energy for you.

Day Six: *Oh Lord, Can Ichabod Be Saved?*

In New England, there is the grave of an old Yankee skinflint. While he was alive, he offered his future heirs their legacy in advance if they would give him 12½ percent interest on it. When he died, they put this epitaph on his tombstone:

Here lies old 12½ percent
The more he saved, the less he spent
The less he spent, the more he saved
Oh Lord, can Ichabod be saved?

Now that's a good question, and it raises a big coping issue: *money*. Many of our fears have to do with money. Those with a lot of it worry about how to invest it or they are fearful about losing it. Those who don't have much, in the extreme, worry about starving. Most of us, in the middle, worry about paying the monthly bills and providing for the future.

Jesus said on one occasion that it was as difficult for a rich man to enter the kingdom of heaven as it was for a camel to go through the eye of a needle. That's a pretty tough saying, isn't it? It is hard, hard for any of us who are in favored positions in life (as most of us are). In fact, no matter how little money we have the likelihood is that we are rich by the world's standards. It's not really a question of how much we have. Money is a coping matter, and most of us have a problem with money.

It's a problem when we don't have enough of it; it's a problem when we have too much of it; it's a problem when we have enough but don't think we have enough. Money is a problem.

But it also offers great potential and great blessing. And that's the reason we need to consider it in the context of coping. I believe that one of the areas in life where we need to learn to cope—but more than to cope, to have a saving perspective—is in the area of material possessions.

Let's begin where Christians should begin, with the scripture.

[Jesus] told them a parable, saying, "The land of a rich man brought forth plentifully; and he thought to himself, 'What shall I do, for I have no where to store my crops?' And he said, 'I will do this: I will pull down my barns, and build larger ones; and there I will store all my grain and my goods. And I will say to my soul, Soul, you have ample goods laid up for many years; take your ease, eat, drink, be merry.' But God said to him, 'Fool! This night your soul is required of you; and the things you have prepared, whose will they be? So is he who lays up treasure for himself, and is not rich toward God.' "

—Luke 12:16–21

Here is a picture of one way to approach money and prosperity. Note two things about this man.

First of all, he never saw beyond himself. That always gets us into trouble. The man never saw beyond himself. There is a proverb that says that money is like seawater—the more a man drinks, the thirstier he becomes. And isn't that the way it is with material possessions?

Think about it in your own life, at whatever level of economic prosperity you may be. The more we drink, the thirstier we become. The more we have, the more we think we need. That's the damnable thing about money and material prosperity. It works subtly and gets a grip upon us. That's not just a problem for the super wealthy. It really is a problem for all of us. The more we get, the more we think we need; the more we have, seemingly the more we want. We seldom look beyond ourselves.

Note another thing about this man: he never saw beyond this world. Listen to him: "I will do this: I will pull down my barns and build larger ones; and I will store all my grain and my goods; and I will say to my soul, Soul, you have ample goods laid up for many years; take your ease, eat, drink, and be merry."

Look at the way you order your life from day to day. Look at your relationships. Is there anything about your living that suggests you might not be here next month—or next year? What kind of treasures are you seeking? Where are you storing your treasure? Are you living as though this were the only world, as though you were going to live forever? Or are you living as though you will not one day face God at a judgment bar and be asked to give an account? Jesus followed his story of the rich farmer with teaching about anxiety and trust (vv. 22–34). Then he closed his teaching by calling us to see life in terms of eternity. "Provide yourselves with purses that do not grow old, with a treasure in the heavens that does not fail, where no thief approaches and no moth destroys. For where your treasure is, there will your heart be also" (Luke 12:33–34).

Reflecting and Recording

In his book, *Prayers,* Michel Quoist has a poignant meditation entitled "Prayer Before a Twenty-Dollar Bill." In it he finds himself thinking about all the different things that little green paper rectangle is capable of accomplishing, and what it may have already accomplished as it has passed from hand to hand to hand.

It's able to buy health care for someone who desperately needs it. Or send a young person to college. It can feed and bless, shelter and make whole, buy trumpets and travel. Or it can prompt someone to rob, to make war. To wreck a world.

Write your own prayer now, expressing your feeling about money—what you have and don't have, what you need, the way you are using your money.

During the Day

Be especially observant today about the role money plays in your life, in your involvement, in the people you meet. Be especially sensitive to pressure points. Try to discover messages that may be coming to you.

Day Seven: *Room When in Distress*

To close this week, and our workbook journey on coping, let's focus on feelings that come from many everyday demands: the feelings of pressure and distress. Psalm 4 deals with the feelings in a very poignant way:

> Answer me when I call, O God of my right!
>> Thou hast given me room when I was in distress.
>> Be gracious to me, and hear my prayer.
>
> O men, how long shall my honor suffer shame?
>> How long will you love vain words and seek after lies? *Selah*
> But know that the Lord has set apart
>> the godly for himself;
>> the Lord hears when I call to him.
>
> Be angry, but sin not;
>> commune with your own hearts on your beds, and be silent. *Selah*
> Offer right sacrifices,
>> and put your trust in the Lord.
>
> There are many who say, "O that we might see some good!
>> Lift up the light of thy countenance upon us, O Lord!"
> Thou hast put more joy in my heart
>> than they have when their grain and wine abound.
>
> In peace I will both lie down and sleep;
>> for thou alone, O Lord, makest me dwell in safety.
>
> —Psalm 4

This psalm provides a model for dealing with distress and pressure from wherever it comes. He talks about the Lord giving him "room when . . . in distress." Isn't that what we need? Relief, space, a way to survive in the midst of pressure.

The psalmist's model provides three directions. First, *face your problem.* Problems do not go away by avoiding them. Rather, the opposite is often true. When we try to avoid problems, they are magnified; in our minds they grow and become more ominous. If we do not acknowledge and face our problems, we never come to the point of bringing these problems to God and receiving God's help.

The psalmist gives us a second direction for finding room when in distress: *Keep a prayer life going and growing.* He put it in a cryptic way in verses 3 and 4: "But know that the Lord has set apart the godly for himself, the Lord hears when I call to him. Be angry, but sin not; commune with your own hearts on your beds, and be silent."

There are two crucial factors about prayer to be underscored here. First, *there are some things God cannot give a person until that person has prepared and proved his or her spirit by persistent prayer.* As Harry Emerson Fosdick reminds us in *The Meaning of Prayer*, "Such praying cleans the house, cleanses the windows, hangs the curtains, sets the table, opens the door, until God says, 'Lo, the house is ready. Now may the guest come in.' "

"Commune with your own hearts on your bed, and be silent." Remember, there are some things God cannot give a person until that person has prepared and proved his or her spirit by persistent prayer.

Now a second factor: Prayer, as the psalmist would teach us, is *conferencing with ourselves.* Many of us use prayer as an escape from ourselves rather than an honest facing of self. In prayer we bring ourselves honestly to ourselves and to God. Ask yourself, for what end was I made? What life have I led? What times have I lost? What love have I abused? What wrath do I deserve?

When we come to God in this fashion, confession is then translated into transformation. We have set the stage for change. Fritz Kunkel, in his book *In Search of Maturity,* makes the point clearly.

Expression of what we find within ourselves, honest and reckless expression before the face of the Eternal, assuming responsibility for what we are, even if we are unaware of it, and asking God to help us to master the wild horses, or to revive the skeletons of horses which we dig out during the long hours of our confessions—this is the psychological method of religious self-education. It is a way of bringing to consciousness our unconscious contents, and of establishing control over our hidden powers. It is the way to mature responsibility. It is the old way of the Psalmist: "Yet who can detect his lapses? Absolve me from my faults unknown! And hold thy servant back from willful sins, from giving way to them" (Psalm 19:12, 13, Moffatt).

Not in the presence of a minister or a psychologist, but in the presence of God, things change completely. If you hate your brother, and you pour out all your hatred, remembering at the same time, as much as you can, the presence of God—and your hatred does not change, then you are not sufficiently aware either of the presence of God or of your hatred, and probably of neither. Be more honest, give vent to your emotions. You hate your brother: imagine his presence, before God tell him how you feel, kick him, scratch him. You are ten years old now—get up from your chair, don't pretend to be a wise old Buddha, pace the floor, yell, scream, punch the furniture, express yourself. Rant and rage until you are exhausted, or until you laugh at yourself (Kunkel, pp. 253–254).

You may think that is extreme. Adjust it to fit your own personality, your own style, but don't miss the point—conference with yourself. "Commune with your own hearts on your beds, and be silent."

The third direction to give us "room when . . . in distress" is a very simple, direct instruction from the psalmist: *Trust in the Lord.* Look at verse 8. "In peace I will both lie down and sleep; for thou alone, O Lord, makest me dwell in safety." How could the psalmist do this? Because he trusted the Lord and could trust the Lord for two reasons.

He remembered the past acts of God. If you want to put it rather crassly, God had always come through for him. That is what he is saying in verse one: "Thou hast given me room when I was in distress."

Not only had the psalmist seen God work in the past, he was confident of God's purpose for his people in the present, so he could trust God. That's what he is saying in verse three: "But know that the Lord has set apart the godly for himself; the Lord hears when I call to him." Note this is *present tense*—"The Lord *hears*."

God gives us room when we are in distress if we trust God. Relief and release may not come immediately, but it will come. Rehearse the lessons the psalmist teaches us:

1. Face your problem.

2. Keep a prayer life going and growing.

3. Trust the Lord.

When we learn these lessons, and practice them, we will always find room in our distress.

Reflecting and Recording

Since this is the last day of your workbook, sit as long as you can, reflecting on this six-week journey. Put down some words or sentences that communicate what you have experienced, questions that have been raised, decisions you have made, directions you have found, truth that has come alive. This is only for you, so make notes that will speak to you, perhaps, a few months from now when you review what you have written here.

During the Day

Make a decision that from this point on you will take some time each day simply to look at your life—especially the problem areas of your life—in the perspective of the promise of Christ, "Lo, I am with you always" (Matt. 28:20).

NOTE: If you are a member of a group sharing this workbook, you will be asked at your meeting to share the meaning of this six-week journey for you: the insights you have received, the questions raised, the changes that have occurred, and the commitments you have made. Take some time before the meeting to review your workbook and make some notes for sharing.

Group Meeting for Week Six

Introduction

This is the last meeting designed for this group. You may have already talked about the possibility of continuing to meet. You should conclude those plans. Some groups find it meaningful to select two or three weeks of the workbook and go through those weeks again as an extension of their time together. Others continue for an additional set time, using other resources. Whatever you choose to do, it is usually helpful to determine the actual time line in order that persons can make a clear commitment.

Another possibility that has been very effective in our congregation in Memphis is for one or two persons to decide they will recruit and lead a group of new persons through this workbook. Many people are looking for a small group growth experience, and this is a way to respond to that need.

Sharing Together

1. Begin by talking about compassion fatigue. Be honest about getting tired of being and doing good.

2. Ask each person to name and describe in two or three sentences one of the persons he/she listed on Day Two who live a compassionate lifestyle.

3. Discuss what prevents us from recognizing and admitting that there is a limit to what we can offer, and why we are often not willing to leave to God and others what we cannot do.

4. Talk about the difference between following Christ and being *in Christ*. Has anyone in the group made the transition? Talk about what you have experienced having made the transition. Though you may not have made the transition completely, have you had experiences when you felt energized because you were *in* Christ? Press the group to be as specific as possible in describing the differences and their related experiences.

5. Ask persons to share their response to spending "selfish" time with people who energize them rather than drain them.

6. Ask persons to indicate their primary coping problem with money.

7. Talk about prayer as conferencing with yourself. Is this a new concept? Who can share experiences of prayer as this dynamic?

8. Use the balance of your discussion time (save time for prayer) for persons to share the meaning of this six-week journey, questions they have, insights they have received, changes that have occurred, commitments they have made.

Praying Together

1. Begin your time of prayer by asking each person to express gratitude to God in a two- or three-sentence prayer for something significant that has happened to him or her as a result of these six weeks.

2. Give each person the opportunity to share whatever decision or commitment he or she has made, or will make, to coping as a Christian. Be specific. Follow each person's verbalizing of these decisions and commitments by having some other person in the group offer a brief prayer of thanksgiving and support for this person.

3. A benediction is a blessing or greeting shared with another or by a group in parting. The "passing of the peace" is such a benediction. You take a person's hand, look into his or her eyes and say, "The peace of God be with you," and the person responds, "And may God's peace be yours." Then that person, taking the hands of the person next to him or her, says "The peace of God be with you," and receives the response, "And may God's peace be yours." Standing in a circle, let the leader "pass the peace," and let it go around the circle.

4. Having completed the passing of the peace, speak to one another in a more spontaneous way. Move about to different persons in the group, saying whatever you feel is appropriate for your parting blessing to each person. Or, you may simply embrace the person and say nothing. In your own unique way, "bless" each person who has shared this journey with you.

Notes

Sources quoted in this workbook are identified in the text by author and page number. If more than one work by the same author is cited, the title of the work is included in the citation Bibliographic information for each source is listed below.

Angell, James W. *Learning to Manage Our Fears.* Nashville: Abingdon, 1981.

Augsberger, Myron. *The Communicator's Commentary,* V. 1. Waco: Word Books, 1982.

Aurandt, Paul. *More of Paul Harvey's The Rest of the Story.* New York: William Morrow, 1980.

Beers, V. Gilbert. "Forgive God?" *Christianity Today,* October 4, 1985.

Council, Raymond J. *Pastoral Psychology* V. 31, 1982.

Dunnam, Maxie. *The Sanctuary for Lent,* March, 1981.

————. *The Sanctuary for Lent,* April, 1983.

Fisher, James T. and S. Hawley Lowell. *A Few Buttons Missing.* Philadelphia: Lippincott, 1951.

Fitzgerald, Ernest A. "It's Alright to Worry," *Piedmont Airlines,* July, 1985.

Forsberg, Clarence. "Even Preachers Get the Blues." Unpublished Sermon. September 5, 1982.

Gore, Robert J. "The Lord *Is* Holding Kirby, After All," *Los Angeles Times,* July 7, 1981.

Hobe, Phyllis. *Coping.* New York: Guideposts, 1983.

Holmes, T. H. and R. H. Rahe. *Journal of Psychomatic Research,* V. 11, 1967.

Hubbard, David Allan. *More Psalms for All Seasons.* Grand Rapids: Eerdmans, 1975.

Johnson, Ben. *You Are Somebody.* Atlanta: Forum House, 1973.

Jordan, Clarence. *The Cotton Patch Version of Paul's Epistles.* New York: Association Press, 1968.

Kennedy, Eugene. *The Pain of Being Human.* Garden City: Image Books, 1974.

Kline, Nathan S. *From Sad to Glad.* New York: Ballantine, 1974.

Kunkel, Fritz. *In Search of Maturity.* New York: Scribner's, 1946.

Miller, Jolonda. *You Can Become Whole Again.* Atlanta: John Knox, 1981.

Moyes, Gordon. *The Secret of Confident Living.* Australia: Vital Publications, 1978.

Ogilvie, Lloyd. *Making Stress Work for You.* Waco: Word Books, 1984.

Palmer, Earl F. *The Communicator's Commentary,* V. 12. Waco: Word Books, 1982.

Paton, Alan. *Too Late the Phalarope.* New York: Scribner's, 1953.

Schmidt, Joseph F. *Praying Our Experiences.* Winona, MN: St. Mary's College Press, 1980.

Spurgeon, C.H. *The Treasury of David,* Vol. I. London: Passmore and Alabaster, 1880.

Stearns, Ann Kaiser. *Living Through Personal Crisis.* New York: Ballantine, 1985.

Wuellner, Flora Slosson. *Prayer, Stress, and Our Inner Wounds.* Nashville: The Upper Room, 1987.

More popular workbooks from

Maxie Dunnam

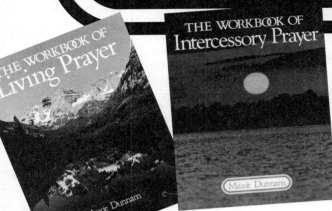

Continue your exploration of the spiritual life with these dynamic workbooks. Each illuminates a unique aspect of devotional living, broadening the user's experience of the power and significance of prayer.

THE WORKBOOK OF LIVING PRAYER is what the name implies. You will not simply read about prayer. You will pray, you will live prayer. No special skills or resources are required.

Weekly themes include: Getting Our Bearings and Beginning the Adventure; With Christ in the School of Prayer; When All Else Fails, Follow the Directions; Basic Ingredients of Prayer and Discovering Your Pattern; Pray without Ceasing; Resources for Praying.

THE WORKBOOK OF INTERCESSORY PRAYER is written with a commitment to the recovery of prayer and relevant spirituality. You don't have to fully understand the power of intercessory prayer to practice it.

Weekly themes include: Getting Intercession into Perspective; Immersing Ourselves in Scripture; Overcoming Some Hurdles; Some Essential Principles of Intercession; Keys for Effective Intercession; Using Imagination and Practicing Non-verbal Prayer; The Intercessor.

THE WORKBOOK ON SPIRITUAL DISCIPLINES helps us see the end toward which discipline takes us—to spiritual growth and maturity in our Christian life and faith.

Weekly themes include: Study, Scripture, and Guidance; Prayer; Confession; Submission and Service; Solitude; Generosity.

THE WORKBOOK ON BECOMING ALIVE IN CHRIST helps Christians explore what it means to be "alive in Christ"—to experience the indwelling Christ as a shaping power in our lives.

Weekly themes include: The Indwelling Christ; Dying and Rising with Christ; An Affirming Presence; A Forgiving and Healing Presence; A Guiding and Creating Presence; A Converting Presence; Being Christ.

Buy copies for yourself and your study group today!

Contact: Your local Christian bookstore

or

Write: **Upper Room Books**
P.O. Box 189
Nashville, TN
37202-0189